Surviving the City

Pacific Formations: Global Relations in Asian and Pacific Perspectives

Series Editor: Arif Dirlik

Surviving the City

The Chinese Immigrant Experience in New York City, 1890–1970

Xinyang Wang

ROWMAN & LITTLEFIELD PUBLISHERS, INC.
Lanham • Boulder • New York • Oxford

ROWMAN & LITTLEFIELD PUBLISHERS, INC.

Published in the United States of America
by Rowman & Littlefield Publishers, Inc.
4720 Boston Way, Lanham, Maryland 20706
www.rowmanlittlefield.com

12 Hid's Copse Road, Cumnor Hill, Oxford OX2 9JJ, England

Copyright © 2001 by Rowman & Littlefield Publishers, Inc.

British Library Cataloging in Publication Information Available

Library of Congress Cataloging-in-Publication Data

Wang, Xinyang, 1947–
Surviving the City : the Chinese immigrant experience in New York City, 1890–1970 / Xinyang Wang.
    p. cm. — (Pacific formations)
    Includes bibliographical references and index.
    ISBN 0-7425-0890-0 (cloth : alk. paper) — ISBN 0-7425-0891-9 (paper : alk. paper)
    1. Chinese Americans—History. 2. Chinese—United States—New York (N.Y.)—Social conditions. I. Title: Chinese immigrant experience in New York City, 1890–1970. II. Title. III. Series.
E184 .C5 W36 2001
974.7'1004951—dc21

2001016215

Printed in the United States of America

♾™ The paper used in this publication meets the minimum requirements of American National Standard for Information Sciences—Permanence of Paper for Printed Library Materials, ANSI/NISO Z39.48-1992.

Contents

Acknowledgements

It is cliché to say that without the help of family, friends, and colleagues it is impossible to complete a book. Nevertheless, I was luckier than many others to enjoy the luxury of being advised by a group of first-rate talents and assisted by a group of the kindest and most devoted people. Knowing and working with these people gave me greater pleasure than even finishing the book itself. Over the years, David Montgomery allowed me to continue sharing his wisdom and insights. I am deeply indebted to Donna Gabaccia who brought to my attention the importance of the ethnic economy in the immigrants' adjustment while I was groping for a theoretical frame work for the book. I am also grateful to Gaochao He who reminded me that the immigrants were rational actors who made choices for their survival.

Two people who unselfishly yet anonymously contributed to the project deserve special mention here. For over ten years, Yimin Lin proved a most loyal friend, exhibiting extraordinary patience and kindness in granting my endless requests. In the meantime, Tron R. Wang served at once as a thoughtful consultant, on-call research assistant, critical reader of the manuscript drafts, and skillful computer programmer. For these two people, to say "I am much obliged" is definitely an understatement.

I wish to express my deep gratitude to Godfrey Harrison who carefully read the entire manuscript and made most detailed and valuable comments. Without these insightful comments, the book would have been of poorer quality. Other people who read the whole or part of the earlier drafts and provided valuable advice include Alexander Hammond, Betty Lee Sung, Susan Armitage, LeRoy Ashby, David Montgomery, Donna Gabaccia, Virginia Unkerfer, Gaochao He, and Cecilia L. F. Chien. They, too, deserve my sincere gratitude.

I wish to thank the following people for providing information and advice: Paul C. Perkus, Susan Klimley, Zhiping Xia, Jowen Tung, Glenda Gilmore, Hasia Diner, Kenneth Terry Jackson, John Kuo Wei Tchen, Mei-ling Liu, and Judith Banister.

viii

I was fortunate to be assisted by a group of unselfish and most efficient library staff at the Hong Kong University of Science & Technology. My thanks go to Shirley Leung, Christina Lo, Louisa Kwok, Eunice Wong, and especially Sau Ping Poon who often went out of her way to help.

Last but definitely not least, I want to thank a group of the best and most conscientious research assistants, some of whom unselfishly reached out their hands when I was in need of help. They did a wonderful job, finding books and journals, checking notes, typing, formatting, and preparing the index. They are Agnes Lai See Ko, Winnie Wing-man Yip, Vinus Wing Shan Fong, Connie Hon Yee Li, Qinghua Cai, Yongbing Zhao, Dorothy Hiu Hung Tse, Kwok-wai Hui, and Alice Wing Shan Shiu. I want to thank Alice especially because she volunteered to help me during perhaps the busiest time of her life. She continued to work hard with great devotion and enthusiasm even when the task turned out to be difficult.

List of Tables

Surviving the City

1

Introduction

America is an immigrant country. All Americans, except Native Americans, are either immigrants or descendants of immigrants. During the century of American industrialization between the 1820s and 1920s, tens of millions of people migrated overseas from Europe and Asia, and overland from Canada and Mexico to the United States.[1] New York City, with its Statue of Liberty beckoning at the poor and the tired, best reflected the situation of the whole country. Many newcomers chose New York as their destination because of the large number and variety of employment opportunities offered in the metropolis. Indeed, few other towns could match New York in terms of the high proportion of immigrant population. According to the 1920 census, almost forty percent of New York City's inhabitants were foreign-born.[2] Though hailing from different shores, the overwhelming majority of the newcomers shared a common goal—to improve their economic lots. Some wished to settle down and to get rich in America. Others came with the idea of earning money to buy land and houses in their home countries. Despite this common goal, however, all the immigrants were not treated equally. Due to their earlier arrival, their numerical strength, and the political power they held, people originally from the British Isles and from western and northern Europe were in a position to set the norm for the country's political, religious, and cultural life. Those from other areas of the world, especially people of color, were often less fortunate, suffering various forms of prejudice and discrimination. Chinese immigrants were long the most discriminated-against group in U.S. history. Even in the early years of the United States when Chinese tea and porcelains were eagerly pursued by elite Americans as symbols of upper-class status, Chinese things, ideas, and people only played a role of inferior "otherness" in shaping European Americans' occidental identity. By the 1880s, the nation's, especially New York's, visual culture had increasingly linked Chinese to rat eating, stereotyping the Chinese with this negative image.[3] For a long time, the United States denied Chinese men the opportunity to immigrate as other men did. Similarly, Chinese men who had arrived before that denial were not allowed to send for their wives. Those

1

who supported U.S. laws against Chinese immigration, attributed deprivations Chinese people suffered to the undesirability of the Chinese race. As we shall see shortly, the Chinese were also the targets of many vicious vilification and violent physical attacks. In light of such a situation, it has been easy to view their adjustment to the American environment solely from the perspective of racial hostilities, or, as scholars did in the early years, solely from the perspective of ethnic heritage. Yet these approaches overlook the crucial role of economic decision making.

This study reassesses the experience of early Chinese immigrants in the United States. Before the late 1970s, most scholars writing about Chinese American history focused on the impact of ethnic heritage on Chinese immigrants' adjustment. There is no doubt that, in crossing the Pacific, Chinese immigrants brought with them their cultural tradition, which later contributed to their adjustment in the United States. But some scholars have considered ethnic heritage as the exclusive factor that affected the immigrants' lives.[4] A typical expression of this line of argument concerns the immigrants' social organizations. Because lineage ties have a long tradition in southeast China, some scholars treated the surname and fellow townsmen's associations among Chinese immigrants simply as replicas of district and lineage organizations common in southeast China.[5] It is true that these organizations in the United States did evolve from the kinship and district networks imported by the Chinese to the United States. But ethnic heritage alone cannot explain why family-name associations—groupings of immigrants sharing the same surname but not necessarily related by blood—became so ubiquitous in Chinese American communities while, in the old country, people seldom formed this kind of organization. It is equally difficult for such an approach to explain why surname organizations were not found among other groups of immigrants, such as the Italians, who also had long traditions of family loyalty.

The ethnic-heritage approach also colored the way these scholars interpreted labor issues. While arguing that Chinese immigrants "became docile subjects of bosses and headmen" in America, one scholar pointed out that the Chinese were "still directed in the United States by the dictates of the Chinese world, sustained by a control system based on family loyalty and fear."[6] This interpretation leaves out mention of any militancy among Chinese laborers. And it, of course, overlooks the facts that Chinese immigrant workers staged several major strikes against their employers in the nineteenth century and even more walkouts during the twentieth. A major drawback of this singular ethnic-heritage approach, obviously, is its neglect of the role played by the American environment, especially discrimination against Chinese, in the immigrants' adjustment. A wider perspective for understanding the experiences of Chinese immigrants became possible toward the end of the 1970s when scholars began focusing attention on the effects of racial hostilities on the newcomers' lives.

A significant contribution to the study of Chinese American history in the past two decades has been the deeper and deeper exploration of the harmful effects of racial discrimination on the adjustment of Chinese immigrants. This discrimination was especially clear in institutionalized racism and anti-Chinese violence. As many recent works of historians, anthropologists, sociologists, and political scientists have shown, Chinese immigrants were victims of the deep-rooted racial discrimination characteristic of nineteenth- and early-twentieth-century America.

Racial prejudice against the Chinese was manifest before the arrival of large groups of Chinese immigrants in California. By the early nineteenth century, American traders, diplomats, and Christian missionaries who had travelled to China had already depicted the Chinese as an inferior, treacherous, and cruel people.[7] A surgeon, who went to China with President Jackson's emissary, observed in the 1830s that China's huge population had made the Chinese "the most vile, the most cowardly and submissive of slaves" and had led to "baseness and extinction of every moral virtue."[8] In the eyes of some missionaries, China was "groaning under an absolute despotism." The Chinese were "venal, tricky, extortionate and cruel." Their "ostentatious kindness" was misleading. "The politeness which they exhibit seldom has its motive in good will, and consequently when the varnish is off, the rudeness, brutality, and coarseness of the material is seen."[9]

California workers were particularly racist toward Chinese immigrants. During the nineteenth century, an important tenet of the ideology of white labor in California was its racial superiority. The idea of racial superiority, as historian Alexander Saxton has demonstrated, severely limited the equality of opportunity in the gold mines. On racial lines, white workers drew a clear distinction between "outsiders" and "insiders." While the English, Scots, Irish, and Germans made up the insiders, Chinese immigrants, together with native Californians (Sonorans) and South Americans, were viewed as outsiders and from inferior races competing with white workers for jobs. Many Chileans, for example, were ousted from the camps because of their failure to pay the state's miners' tax. But the Chinese turned out to be the principal victims of mob attacks and discriminatory laws.[10]

In 1850, in response to white miners' demand, California passed a piece of legislation called the Foreign Miners' License Tax Law that required every foreign miner unwilling to become a U.S. citizen to pay three dollars a month. Although nominally aimed at all foreign miners, Chinese immigrants became the chief losers under this act because they were non-white and were always treated as aliens. By 1870 when the law was repealed, the Chinese had lost five million dollars—money they never retrieved.[11] In the mid-1850s, a notorious legal case set a precedent of barring the Chinese from effectively using the U.S. court system. In 1853, Ling Sing, a Chinese immigrant, was murdered. George Hall, the chief suspect, was prosecuted and tried. During the court hearings, three Chinese and one white testified against the suspect. Hall was subsequently found guilty and received a death sentence. But his attorney challenged the verdict by referring to a California law that stipulated that blacks and Indians could not testify in favor of or against whites in court. The judge eventually reversed the verdict in 1854 and, in the legal decision *People v. Hall*, the California Supreme Court ruled that the Chinese could not testify in court.[12] This ruling reinforced other denials of Chinese immigrants' equality in American society. These other denials included school segregation and anti-miscegenation laws.[13]

White workers' hatred toward Chinese immigrants triggered a series of violent anti-Chinese acts throughout the western states. Dozens of Chinese were killed, hundreds were assaulted, and the survivors' losses of property were inestimable. A particularly brutal anti-Chinese attack took place in Rock Springs, Wyoming, in 1885. The 331 Chinese then living in Rock Springs were miners employed by the Union Pacific Railroad Company. In September 1885, a dispute between Chinese and white miners over who should work which part of the mine triggered the riot. A mob of 150 armed men surrounded the Chinese quarter and fired at the helpless Asians. Altogether twenty-eight Chinese were killed and fifteen wounded.[14] Late-nineteenth-century massacres of Chinese immigrants also occurred in Los Angeles, Portland, Tacoma, Seattle, and Denver.[15]

The anti-Chinese movements on the West Coast culminated in the Chinese Exclusion Act of 1882. As mentioned earlier, Chinese laborers were the first, and for a long time the only, group singled out by an immigration law as racially undesirable. With the exception of merchants, students, tourists, and diplomats, the Chinese Exclusion Act prohibited Chinese laborers from entering the United States for the next ten years. It also forbade naturalization of the Chinese already in the country.[16] As a matter of fact, the 1790 Naturalization Law, which stipulated that only white males could become U.S. citizens, had already deprived the Chinese of the right of naturalization.[17] Because some states did not vigorously enforce this law, quite a few Chinese became U.S. citizens in the nineteenth century.[18] After the passage of the Chinese Exclusion Act, no opportunity for the Chinese to become naturalized remained. Like others, Chow Fo was a New York Chinese who became a U.S. citizen in 1879 only to be de-naturalized by the U.S. District Court in New York. In 1911, it ruled that Chow was not a free white person and so could not be a naturalized citizen of the United States.[19] The baneful effects of the Exclusion Act were obvious. Disfranchised Chinese immigrants had no electoral or directly democratic means to employ in the hope of righting the wrongs they had suffered. Legislation enforced by court rulings had rendered them a minority, already tiny, devoid of practical political influence.

The rights of Chinese immigrants were further curtailed by the Scott Act of 1888. According to this act, once a Chinese left the United States, he could not reenter the country. Since the law did not provide the victims a grace period, twenty thousand Chinese immigrants with reentry permits were denied landing after visiting their families in China.[20] In 1892, Congress passed a law known as the Geary Act that extended the Chinese Exclusion Act for ten years. In 1902, a congressional decree authorized further, indefinite extension of Chinese exclusion. In addition to robbing Chinese Americans of political rights there, these exclusion laws deprived Chinese women of the right to join their husbands in the United States. Consequently, for more than six decades, the Chinese American community was basically a bachelor's society. Not until 1943 did Congress repeal the Exclusion Act as a special effort to befriend China, a U.S. ally during World War II.

The emphasis on considering the effects of racial hostilities widens our perspective for understanding some important issues in Chinese American history. Taking into account the lack of women among the Chinese immigrants as a result of the exclusion laws, for example, allows us to understand better why the Chinese eventually formed family-name associations: In a hostile environment, the helpless bachelors had no other choice but to extend the meaning of "family" by recruiting all people with the same surname into a quasi-family organization for mutual assistance. Similarly, hostilities in the established unions often prevented the Chinese from joining the organized American labor movement. As we shall see in chapter 6, the two national labor unions—the Knights of Labor and the American Federation of Labor—not only denied Chinese immigrant workers the privilege of joining the movement but also refused to assist the Asians when the latter struck.

The effects of institutionalized racism and anti-Chinese violence on the lives of Chinese immigrants in America definitely deserve further exploration. Even so, there is a risk in understanding the history of Chinese immigrants always as a history of victims. We risk portraying these people, people who sustained their culture and overcame the contrived strictures of a society to which they contributed but that persisted in stigmatizing them, as puppets or automata. Such a portrayal would be a travesty of the history of those Chinese whose lives of suffering, hardship, endurance, adaptation, achievement, and even triumph are at the core of that migration we seek to illuminate and understand.

The tendency of portraying the Chinese only as victims often results from isolating the effects of racial hostilities from other factors affecting the immigrants' adjustments. As we shall see shortly, there are some important issues that a racial-hostilities-only approach can not fully explain. One such issue is the return migration pattern followed by the Chinese. Undoubtedly, the discriminatory laws and anti-Chinese violence made it extremely difficult, if not virtually impossible, for the Chinese to live a normal and peaceful life, let alone to become rich, in the United States. Consequently, to return to their home villages with their savings became the only practical option for the Chinese immigrants. It is common knowledge that, despite some degree of improvement during World War II, discrimination against the Chinese in America remained severe until the 1960s. Life was especially hard for Chinese immigrants during the Korean War in the early 1950s when they were placed under strict surveillance. If racial hostility had been the only factor affecting Chinese adjustment in the United States, then the immigrants should have continued to return to China. But why did they suddenly reverse their "sojourner" mentality in the early 1950s and decide to stay in America?

Also deserving our attention is the problem of Chinese immigrants' residential location preferences. Some scholars have assumed that to avoid housing discrimination and harassment in the white neighborhoods and to be close to a familiar culture, the overwhelming majority of Chinese immigrants lived in Chinatown most of the time.[21] But this assumption cannot explain the realities of New York City. There increasing numbers of Chinese chose to live in "white" neighborhoods and did so from the 1890s to the 1950s even while housing discrimination and harassment against them were rampant.

One may very well suppose that discrimination from the larger society should push Chinese immigrants to suppress their regional and kinship loyalties and to seek long-term community unity.[22] Again, this does not seem to have been the case for the New York Chinese. Before the 1960s, regional and kinship loyalties so predominated the daily life of the New York Chinese that even the need to save their motherland China and to fight racial discrimination only intermittently convinced the Chinese to subdue their group allegiances.

Similarly, hostilities of the established labor unions have been recognized by conventional wisdom as the reason for Chinese immigrant workers' aloofness from trade unionism. This interpretation, however, cannot help us understand the occasions when certain established labor unions, rather than showing hostility, did approach the New York Chinese though the Chinese themselves were still reluctant to join them. Last but not least, racial hostilities alone may not fully explain why group allegiance declined earlier and labor militancy developed faster among the San Francisco Chinese than among the New York Chinese. Apparently, we need to explore new perspectives to have a comprehensive understanding of these issues.

Some recent studies of U.S. immigration history remind us of the essential role played by the "ethnic economy" in the immigrants' lives. Edna Bonacich and John Modell's study of the Japanese American community demonstrates that the way an ethnic group organized their economy was a key to understanding the immigrants' adjustment in the United States.[23] Their study reveals a close link between small-business concentration and ethnic solidarity. Japanese enterprise owners mostly employed their compatriots who were more loyal to the firms than to labor unions.[24] Economic factors were also important in the life of the second-generation Japanese Americans, although to a lesser extent: Those involved in the ethnic economy were more likely to maintain close relationships with their co-ethnics than those who did not participate in small businesses.[25]

This economic/sociological argument of immigration distinguishes between two kinds of ethnic economies: concentration in small businesses (or the middlemen groups) and ethnic enclaves. The characteristics of a middlemen group include, among others, the tendency to return to the home country, dispersal of residences among other populations, and group loyalties along locality and kinship lines.[26] An enclave economy does not involve those traits. It is composed of clustered networks of businesses owned by members of the ethnic group. Enclave economies are diversified with both industrial production and specialized services. The emergence and success of an enclave economy often depend on the influx of capital from the home country and on co-ethnics for an essential supply of workers and market. As we shall see in the following chapters, in the case of the pre-1965 New York Chinese, there were indeed close links between small business concentration, return migration, dispersal of the immigrants' residences, continuation of group loyalties, and a lack of labor militancy. After 1965, when concentration in small businesses gave way to an enclave economy, the adjustment patterns of the New York Chinese began to change as well. Now more and more of them clustered in Chinatown, their group loyalties began to weaken, and they began to identify themselves with the American labor movement.

Recently, some historians have suggested that the desire to purchase land at home motivated both European and Chinese peasants to migrate to the United States. It follows that most immigrants would have originated from areas where land was widely distributed and available for sale and in fact most did.[27] Along this line, the book further suggests that it is necessary to compare the economic opportunities available to the Chinese on each side of the Pacific. Such a comparison offers a means to understand why the Chinese continued to return home from the late nineteenth century through the 1940s, and why in the early 1950s they abruptly reversed their sojourner mentality. Before the 1950s, their employment and business opportunities in small laundries and restaurants promised no hope of upward mobility in American society. To return home to become small landholders was therefore always attractive to the Chinese. In the early 1950s, when economic opportunities in the United States appeared slightly better than those in Guangdong where land purchased by the potential returnees had been confiscated, Chinese immigrants decided to stay in America despite continued racial discrimination against them there.

The ethnic economy approach is also helpful for understanding the issues concerning the immigrants' residential location choices. The concentration of the New York Chinese in the laundry and restaurant industries explains why more and more of them took up residence in the white neighborhoods before the 1960s. As this study shows, Chinese laundries and restaurants in New York had to be scattered to be close to enough mainly white customers. Because the immigrant workers always wished to live close to their workplaces, increasing numbers of New York Chinese moved to live in white neighborhoods despite housing discrimination and harassment there.

The workplace situation was a key to sustaining group loyalties alongside hindering class consciousness among Chinese immigrant workers. Before the 1960s, the small size of Chinese firms—laundries and restaurants—often enabled their owners to hire their fellow townsmen or kinsmen exclusively. As a result, the New York Chinese had no opportunities to mix with workers from different kinship or regional backgrounds. The situation at the workplace thereby tended to strengthen the immigrants' regional or kinship loyalties and encouraged employer-worker collaboration rather than class consciousness or working-class solidarity. Therefore, the New York Chinese remained unresponsive when some established labor unions approached them and urged them to join the movement.

In brief, racial hostilities were not the only factor affecting Chinese immigrants' adjustment: The immigrants had to survive economic hardships as well as to endure anti-Chinese violence and institutionalized racism. The assumption that anti-Chinese violence and institutionalized racism were more harmful and more unbearable than other forms of injustice will ineluctably lead to the conclusion that Chinese continued to return to Guangdong in the 1950s, clustered in Chinatown to avoid outside discrimination, and, for the sake of community unity, tended to subdue their group loyalties. But, as the following chapters show, Chinese immigrants' efforts to survive the two different kinds of hardships—both social and economic—led them to tactics and adaptations more subtle than either form of hardship might alone require. Often, they had to choose a lesser evil from several options, of which none was perfect. In order to make a living, for example, many New York Chinese had to endure the housing discrimination and harassment their white neighbors devised against them. For these Chinese to stay in Chinatown would have been to exchange such injustices for the hardship of extreme poverty. Similarly, to survive economic hardships, the Chinese had to maintain their group allegiances even though the need to fight other forms of injustice required the abandonment of such loyalties.

New York City was selected for this study because the history of New York's Chinese community has received less attention than California's. Fortunately, the past two decades have brought us several books that deal with the Chinese community in New York before 1965. Peter Kwong's *Chinatown New York: Labor and Politics, 1930-1950* (1979) discusses the labor movement and politics in the New York Chinese community. By calling attention to the effects of China's weakness on the Chinese American community, the book opens a new and useful perspective for understanding the history of Chinese immigrants in New York City. John Kuo-wei Tchen's *New York Before Chinatown: Orientalism and the Shaping of American Culture, 1776-1882* (1999) traces the evolution of the anti-Chinese racial discourse in New York City prior to the formation of Chinatown in the 1880s. The book illustrates how different forms of orientalism were at work: While patrician orientalism asserted elite Americans' social status, commercial orientalism enabled the distorted and negative image of the Chinese to reach a much larger audience. Renqiu Yu's *To Save China, To Save Ourselves: The Chinese Hand Laundry Alliance of New York* (1992) is a welcome case study of a group of Chinese laundrymen in New York City in the 1930s and 1940s. These works, of course, illuminate the history of the New York Chinese. Their success, however, makes more stark how little we yet know of the return migration, residential location choices, group allegiances, and the role played by the artisans among the New York Chinese. These surely worthwhile themes all involve questions that an ethnic-economy perspective looks suited to throw light upon and so better and more fully illuminate the history of the New York Chinese.

To place the history of the New York Chinese in a broader perspective, we shall briefly consider the experience of the Italian immigrants in New York. The substantial headway in the study of American immigration history over recent years has necessarily left the discussion of comparative themes less well developed than its appraisals of events within communities. This relatively small contribution is especially so for comparisons of Chinese immigrants and those from eastern and southern Europe. Because of the lack of comparative studies, we lack detailed knowledge and often have only theoretical perspectives about the differing and similar experiences of Asian and European immigrants and factors (beyond legal discrimination) that contributed to the unique adjustment patterns of Asian and European immigrants in particular communities. While comparative perspectives have their limitations, they yield particular benefits for the study of Chinese immigrant history. For example, historians have found that the role played by artisans had a crucial effect on the adjustment of European immigrants. These skilled workers not only had a strong intention to settle permanently in the New World but also led the peasant immigrants in demonstrating interest in the labor movement and American politics, but this remains a relatively unexplored area in the history of Chinese immigration. The following chapters draw on the Italian experience to show the importance of the effects of economic discrimination, especially in the workplace, and the role played by immigrant artisans.

Many similarities between the Chinese and the Italian immigrant groups encourage our use of the Italian experience as a point of reference to inform our more detailed consideration of the Chinese one. Both groups, for example, had largely rural backgrounds, were regarded by the larger society as "birds of passage" unwilling to sink roots in the United States, were subjected to housing and job discrimination, and were the butts of derogatory comparisons with each other. Indeed, politicians, reformers, and labor leaders frequently referred to the Italians as "the Chinese of Europe."[28] So, too, did Italian immigrants, like Chinese ones, arrive in New York in relatively large numbers during the 1880s.[29] This investigation thus begins with 1890, the year when Little Italys and Chinatown became salient features of the city's life.

Yet the two immigrant groups followed markedly different adjustment patterns in New York City. In migrating to the United States, many Italians chose to settle in New York because the city offered plenty of employment opportunities for European immigrants. In contrast, it was to California, not to New York, that large groups of Chinese had originally migrated. The need for labor in building the railroad and reclaiming swampy land meant that the Chinese were welcomed at first. Before long they found this welcome had vanished and they were targets for racial hatred and of discriminatory laws. In the face of racial hostility, many Chinese began to disperse to other parts of the country. Some who hoped to avoid the harsh treatment they had received in California or other western states migrated to New York. Demographically, the New York Chinese community was always much smaller than its Italian counterpart. By the end of World War I, the New York Italian community had grown to almost one million. By contrast, until the 1950s, racist immigration laws kept the Chinese community between 2,000 and 13,000, with very few women and children.

For a long time, Italian immigrants were also discriminated against by the larger society. Hostility against the Italians was almost as widespread as that against the Chinese. In 1895, in the coal mines of Colorado, six Italians were murdered, and in 1900, another four. In the twenty years between 1891 and 1910, thirty-two Italians in five southern states were killed in mob lynchings. In the year 1891 alone, eleven Italian immigrants were lynched.[30] Like their Chinese counterparts, too, many Italian immigrants encountered discrimination while looking for housing and employment. In commenting on the discrimination toward Italian immigrants, *Bollettino della Sera*, an Italian newspaper published in New York City, pointed out in the early twentieth century that "the Italians bade fair to be classed with the Chinese."[31] But there existed a fundamental difference between the discrimination against Chinese and that against Italian immigrants. Italian immigrants, no matter how severely discriminated against by the larger society, were white and retained the privilege of becoming naturalized as U.S. citizens. Once naturalized, they could vote to negotiate with the larger society for the improvement of their conditions. Besides, politicians often could not afford to ignore Italians' growing numerical strength. By contrast, the discrimination against the far less numerous Chinese had few political costs, domestic or international. As said earlier, by the end of the nineteenth century, discrimination against the Chinese had become institutionalized.

New York City could arguably claim relatively more racial tolerance toward Chinese immigrants than California. For example, no large-scale anti-Chinese movements took place there as they did in many western cities although that fact could simply be the result of the small number of Chinese immigrants living in New York. In addition, there were no anti-miscegenation laws in New York State; therefore, we find examples of intermarriage between Chinese men and

Caucasian women in that city. This does not imply, however, that chances for Chinese immigrants to marry white women were abundant. In most cases, racial and cultural barriers still made intermarriage an impossibility. In San Francisco Chinese children went to a Chinese-only school; in New York school segregation was not imposed on the Chinese. In fact, Chinese and Italian children attended the same public school—Public School No. 23—in the Lower East Side.

But although in terms of suffering from violence and harassment the Chinese fared slightly better in New York than in California, they were everywhere subject to the Exclusion Act. Newspapers in New York, moreover, kept smearing Chinese throughout the nineteenth century and well into the twentieth. Economically, the New York Chinese fared even worse than their brethren on the West Coast. Although the anti-Chinese movement drove many California Chinese out of mining and manufacturing, a substantial minority of the San Francisco Chinese continued to work in cigarmaking, shoemaking, and clothing industries in the late nineteenth and early twentieth centuries—different work from that restaurants and laundries offered the New York Chinese from the 1880s to the 1960s. Chinese garment factories, furthermore, came into existence in the 1870s and became a leading industry in San Francisco's Chinatown as early as the 1920s. As we shall see, the different occupational opportunities may have contributed to the dissimilar adjustment patterns of the two Chinese communities.

Italian immigrants were treated better in California than in New York, a fact that their smaller numbers in the West may explain. Italians in California were also older on the average than their brethren in the East Coast cities. In California, furthermore, the Chinese and other Asians were made a common enemy. As a partial consequence, Italian workers, being white, were saved from much harassment.[32] In New York, Italians were a relatively large proportion of the city's labor force and the fewer Chinese were excluded from its mainstream labor market. In this setting, Italians became the more visible target of American nativism.[33] To say that the Chinese somehow fared a little better in New York than in California does not at all mean they were necessarily treated as the equals of European immigrants. In many ways, they were still much less fortunate than their Italian counterparts.

After World War I, New York Italians had gradually overcome their group loyalties and joined the American labor movement. The Chinese did not take positions equivalent to the Italians' until the late 1960s. At that time, the civil rights movement pulled down a number of the racial barriers that impeded the New York Chinese community, and the emergence of an enclave economy led the New York Chinese to new relationships in their workplaces.

The Immigration Act of 1965 ended the national-origin quotas the 1924 law had stipulated, and U.S. immigration policy became based on a more reasonable principle—those who wished to immigrate to the United States were to be admitted, or not, on the basis of their skills and their having close relatives living in the country. This liberal immigration law gave fresh impetus to the demographic increase in the New York Chinese community that had been under way since 1943, when Congress repealed the Chinese Exclusion Act. After 1965, the new immigrants to New York often came as nuclear families. Many newcomers since the 1960s hailed from Hong Kong instead of rural Guangdong. These new immigrants often had ranges of skills and attitudes toward trade unionism that differed from those of their predecessors from Guangdong. In the 1960s, too, many older-generation Chinese immigrants, especially laundrymen, had begun to retire, and a sizeable "second" generation of Chinese Americans was coming of age. These changes and the work discontinuities that resulted explain why this investigation ends with the year 1970.

By the late 1960s, some important changes also took place in the economic life of New York Chinese. Coupled with the thousands of new immigrants, capital from Hong Kong and Taiwan also poured into New York's Chinatown. These new conditions led to the rise of an ethnic enclave economy in Chinatown. The garment factories, which gained importance in the Chinatown economy in the 1960s, each employed dozens of workers. The much bigger workplace made it difficult for the employers to hire only their fellow townsmen or kinsmen. For the first time immigrants from different regional and kinship backgrounds had an opportunity to mingle together and to develop camradarie at the workplace. These shifts hastened the decline of the immigrants' group loyalties while conversely promoting their class consciousness. A few specialized works have addressed particular aspects of this transformation, although additional studies will further detail and assess the full range of the post-1965 transformation within the New York Chinese community.[34] Although the pre-1965 period is the main concern of this book, the investigation goes several years beyond that point to end with the year 1970 to demonstrate the major changes that occurred for the New York Chinese community during the late 1960s.

Before ending this introduction, I would like to make an observation on the sources of this study. I explored primary sources for the history of Italian immigration only to the extent needed to employ the Italian experience as a point of reference. Readers will realize that I do not attempt to exhaust all the secondary sources on Italian immigration and I refrain from doing so for the same reason. For the study of the New York Chinese, however, the arguments rest mainly on primary sources. I rely heavily on the newspapers from immigrant presses in New York City. The six Chinese language newspapers, *Guo Quan Bao (The Chinese Republic News)*, *Wei Xin Bao (The Chinese Reform News)*, *Min Qi Ri Bao (The Chinese Nationalist Daily)*, *Xian Feng Bao (The Chinese Vanguard)*, *Mei Zhou Hua Qiao Ri Bao (China Daily News)*, and *Xin Bao (China Tribune)*, had either remained unexplored or had been explored for other purposes than mine. Besides reading these newspapers page by page, I consulted government census data, immigration commission reports, Chinese Exclusion files, publications by the New York Chinese organizations, and such English newspapers and magazines published in New York as the *New York Times*, the *New York Tribune*, and *Harper's Weekly*. All English quotations from Chinese language sources are my translations.

Notes

1. During the decade of 1901-1910 alone, more than 8.7 million people migrated to the United States. See Leonard Dinnerstein, Roger L. Nichols and David M. Reimers, *Natives and Strangers: Ethnic Groups and the Building of America* (New York: Oxford University Press, 1979), 122-23.

2. United States Government, U.S. Bureau of the Census, *The Fourteenth Census, 1920*, Vol. III (Washington, D.C.: Government Printing House, 1922), 710.

3. John Kuo-wei Tchen, *New York Before Chinatown: Orientalism and the Shaping of American Culture, 1776-1882* (Baltimore, Md.: The Johns Hopkins University Press, 1999), especially 54-130 and 260-78.

4. Gunther Barth, for example, has written that Chinese immigrants "clung tenaciously to their culture and rejected the new standards." See Gunther Barth, *Bitter Strength: A History of the Chinese in the United States, 1850-1870* (Cambridge, Mass.: Harvard University Press, 1964), 5.

5. Virginia Heyer, "Patterns of Social Organizations in New York's Chinatown" (Ph.D. dissertation, Columbia University, 1953), 54.

6. Barth, *Bitter Strength*, 212.

7. Stuart C. Miller, *The Unwelcome Immigrant: The American Image of the Chinese, 1785-1882* (Berkeley: University of California Press, 1969), 16-80.

8. Miller, *The Unwelcome Immigrant*, 27.

9. Miller, *The Unwelcome Immigrant*, 72.

10. Alexander Saxton, *The Indispensable Enemy: Labor and the Anti-Chinese Movement in California* (Berkeley: University of California Press, 1971), 52.

11. Roger Daniels, *Asian America: Chinese and Japanese in the United States since 1850* (Seattle: University of Washington Press, 1988), 33; Ronald Takaki, *Strangers from a Different Shore: A History of Asian Americans* (Boston: Little, Brown and Company, 1989), 81-82.

12. Daniels, *Asian America*, 34; Takaki, *Strangers from a Different Shore*, 102.

13. Sucheng Chan, *Asian Americans: An Interpretive History* (Boston: Twayne Publishers, 1991), 57-58; Takaki, *Strangers from a Different Shore*, 101-02.

14. Daniels, *Asian America*, 61-62.

15. Elmer Clarence Sandmeyer, *The Anti-Chinese Movement in California* (Urbana, Ill.: University of Illinois Press, 1973), 48, 97; Chan, *Asian Americans*, 48-51; Daniels, *Asian America*, 58-66.

16. The complete title of this law was "An Act to Execute Certain Treaty Stipulations Relating to Chinese." See William L. Tung, *The Chinese in America, 1820-*

14 Chapter 1

1973: A Chronology & Fact Book (Dobbs Ferry, N.Y.: Oceana Publications, 1974), 58, 61.

17. Takaki, *Strangers from a Different Shore*, 82.

18. Sucheng Chan, "European and Asian Immigration into the United States in Comparative Perspective, 1820s to 1920s," in *Immigration Reconsidered: History, Sociology, and Politics*, ed. Virginia Yans-McLaughlin (New York: Oxford University Press, 1990), 65. For more examples of naturalization of New York Chinese, see Arthur Bonner, *Alas! What Brought Thee Hither? The Chinese in New York, 1800-1950* (Madison: Fairleigh Dickinson University Press, 1997), 17, 44, 48, and Tchen, *New York Before Chinatown*, 76, 136, 231-32, 247.

19. "The United States vs. Chow Fo," in *Chinese Exclusion Files*, kept in the National Archives, New York Public Library.

20. Chan, *Asian Americans*, 55.

21. For a long time, scholars who examined the residential situation of the New York Chinese focused on Chinatown and emphasized a common culture and racial hostility in pushing the Chinese to live in the enclave. See D. Y. Yuan, "Voluntary Segregation: A Study of New York Chinatown," *Phylon: Atlanta University Review of Race and Culture* (fall 1963), 255-65; and Yvonne M. Lau, "Traditionalism and Change in a Chinese American Community," in *The Chinese in America*, ed. Paul K.T. Sih and Leonard B. Allen (New York: St. Johns University Press, 1976), 116. Basing one's argument just on these two factors will naturally lead to the conclusion that most Chinese lived in Chinatown most of the time. Min Zhou, for example, thinks that most New York Chinese had lived in Manhattan's Chinatown before the 1960s. See Zhou, *Chinatown: The Socioeconomic Potential of an Urban Enclave* (Philadelphia: Temple University Press, 1992), 186.

22. Chia-ling Kuo, *Social and Political Change in New York's Chinatown* (New York: Praeger, 1977), 18, 28.

23. Edna Bonacich and John Modell, *The Economic Basis of Ethnic Solidarity: Small Business in the Japanese American Community* (Berkeley: University of California Press, 1980), 3-4.

24. Bonacich and Modell, *The Economic Basis of Ethnic Solidarity*, 51.

25. Bonacich and Modell, *The Economic Basis of Ethnic Solidarity*, 187-216.

26. Bonacich and Modell, *The Economic Basis of Ethnic Solidarity*, 15; Alejandro Portes, *The Economic Sociology of Immigration: Essays on Networks, Ethnicity, and Entrepreneurship* (New York: Russell Sage Foundation, 1995), 27.

27. See Chan, "European and Asian Immigration into the United States in Comparative Perspective," 38-44.

28. President Woodrow Wilson was probably the first person to use this term. Newspapers and magazines often put Italian and Chinese together in their editorials and commentaries.

29. Although both Italian and Chinese immigrants began to settle in New York City decades before the American Civil War, the peasant immigrants, the main object of this study, did not migrate to New York in large numbers until the 1880s.

30. See Robert D. Parmet, *Labor and Immigration in Industrial America* (Boston: Twayne Publishers, 1981), 129-36.

31. *Bollettino della Sera*, 30 March 1908. Quoted in Robert E. Park and Herbert A. Miller, *Old World Traits Transplanted* (New York: Harper & Brothers Publishers, 1921), 252.

32. See Micaela di Leonardo, *The Varieties of Ethnic Experience: Kinship, Class, and Gender among California Italian Americans* (Ithaca, N.Y.: Cornell University Press, 1984), 56-57, 64; Daniels, *Asian America*, 33.

33. For a discussion of how Italians in other cities fared better than their counterparts in New York, see Samuel L. Baily, "The Adjustment of Italian Immigrants in Buenos Aires and New York, 1870-1914," *The American Historical Review*, Vol. 88, No. 2 (April 1983), 281-305, especially 291-92 and 298-99.

34. These works include, among others, Peter Kwong's books *The New Chinatown* (New York: Hill and Wang, 1987) and *Forbidden Workers: Illegal Chinese Immigrants and American Labor* (New York: New Press, 1997); Betty Lee Sung's *The Adjustment Experience of Chinese Immigrant Children in New York City* (New York: Center for Migration Studies, 1987); Hsiang-shui Chen's *Chinatown No More: Taiwan Immigrants in Contemporary New York* (Ithaca, N.Y.: Cornell University Press, 1992); and Min Zhou's *Chinatown: The Socioeconomic Potential of an Urban Enclave* (Philadelphia: Temple University Press, 1992).

2

Artisans and Peasants from Guangdong

Chinese immigrants began to arrive in the United States long before the American Civil War. Legend has it that a Chinese monk named Hui Shen sailed to north America in A.D. 459. The Buddhist priest together with his entourage allegedly landed at what appeared to be the present-day California and, upon his return, wrote a detailed record of the flora he found there.[1] Though the legend remains unsubstantiated, there is no denying the fact that in 1849, the year of the Gold Rush, the several thousand adventurers who had arrived in San Francisco already included 325 Chinese.[2] In the following year, the Chinese participated in the ceremony for California's entry into the Union. They were told by Justice Nathaniel Bennett that though born and raised under different governments they would be treated as equals in the Golden State. In 1852, the celebration of President George Washington's birthday was joined by some two hundred Chinese whom a visitor described as the "most orderly and industrious citizens." In an address to the state lawmakers, California governor John McDougal emphasized the need for more Chinese immigrants to reclaim the swampy lands there and eulogized the Chinese as "one of the most worthy classes of our newly adopted citizens."[3]

The early California Chinese were probably preceded by their fellow countrymen who set foot in eastern American cities no later than 1847. In that year, if we believe anecdotes, when the junk *Keying*, a Chinese vessel commanded by an Australian captain, anchored in the harbor off lower Manhattan, its Chinese crew allegedly jumped ship and started the New York Chinese community.[4] Some recent scholarship dates the arrival of Chinese in New York City even decades earlier than the visit of *Keying*. The burgeoning China trade in the beginning of the nineteenth century hastened the rise of New York as a leading port and, coupled with the China trade, the coming and going of Chinese sailors led to the formation of what might be the first Chinese American community.[5] Despite this early arrival, few Chinese migrated directly from China to New York before the 1880s. In 1880, only 747 Chinese immigrants lived in the city.[6] As mentioned earlier, it was to California, not to New York, that large groups of Chinese had originally emigrated. The discovery of gold in California in 1848 had provided white adventurers with opportunities to get rich quickly. That prospect lured Chinese to immigrate to the United States in the late 1840s. In the early years, most Chinese were independent placer miners. Spending many hours by the river each day, they used pans to patiently sift out sand from gold. Although they could only work the poor and cheap claims abandoned by white miners, some Chinese did manage to build small fortunes, which encouraged more fellow countrymen to cross the Pacific in the 1850s. The 1860 census counted 34,933 Chinese in the United States.[7]

During the 1860s and 1870s, the construction of the transcontinental railroad heightened the need for cheap labor, providing a further boost for Chinese immigration. The Central Pacific Railroad Company, whose task was to lay tracks eastward from Sacramento, had engaged white laborers initially. But the rough working conditions, especially those in the Sierras, deterred white workingmen and most quit immediately when brought to the railhead.[8] In the 1860s, European Americans were still too enamored of working the mines to show interest in railroad construction. Yet, competition for railroad construction was intense as the bounty offered by Congress—6,400 acres of gratuitous land for each mile of tracks laid—was irresistible.[9] Already, the Union Pacific Railroad Company, Central Pacific's chief rival, was moving faster in building tracks westward from Omaha. Relying on easy access to labor and materials by way of the Missouri River, the Union Pacific reportedly laid tracks at the speed of one mile a day, beating the Central Pacific eight to one.[10] Beset by labor shortages, the Central Pacific decided to give Chinese laborers a try. To the surprise of many people who at first doubted the capabilities of the Chinese, the latter proved to be sturdy workers whose industry, ingenuity, and perseverance soon enabled the company to catch up with the Union Pacific. Although paid less than white workers, the Chinese undertook the most difficult job assignments. Often they had to drill holes in granite rocks while standing in wicker baskets lowered by ropes from the top of cliffs. Then, they put dynamite into the holes and lit the fuses before being raised to the peak by fellow workers. This task involved even more hazards because those who failed to move away quickly were killed in the explosions. Heavy casualties also resulted from avalanches that buried many Chinese at work—sometimes an entire crew— without prior warning. In most cases, bodies of the dead could not be found until the following spring when the snow melted.[11] For all the dangers and difficulties, the Chinese moved faster than employers expected. No wonder the engineer in charge of the project described the Chinese as "the best roadbuilders in the world."[12] Leland Stanford, first president of the Central Pacific, also lauded the Chinese in a report to President Andrew Johnson in 1865:

As a class, they are quiet, peaceable, patient, industrious, and economical. More prudent and economical [than white laborers] they are contented with less wages. Without them, it would be impossible to complete the western portion of this great national enterprise within the time required by the Act of Congress.[13]

In subsequent years, the Central Pacific reached out to more and more Chinese workers, ex-miners in California as well as potential emigrants in southeast China. The number of Chinese on the company's payroll jumped from fifty in 1858 to about eleven thousand in the late 1860s.[14]

Other events also contributed to the influx of Chinese immigrants into California. In 1868, China and the United States reached an agreement on immigration matters that became known as the Burlingame Treaty. By signing this pact, the Qing government finally recognized the right of the Chinese people to emigrate to America, ending the three-hundred-year ban on overseas migration.[15] Now those who wanted to go abroad no longer had to worry about any punishments. They could emigrate openly and freely. The United States, on the other hand, was obligated to allow the Chinese to work and reside in America. Increasing the convenience of travelling to California was the new steamboat line between Hong Kong and San Francisco, opened by the Pacific Mail Steamship Company in 1867.[16] By the early 1880s, thousands of Chinese had taken advantage of these conveniences in migrating to America. The number of Chinese in the United States reached its zenith for that century: More than 100,000 Chinese were in the United States in 1880.[17]

In California, the Chinese worked in manufacturing as well as mining, agriculture, and railroad construction. In 1880, for example, California's Chinese working population included 22 percent laborers, 20 percent miners, and 15 percent farm workers. Less then a third of them were in the service industry.[18] In the same year, cigarmakers, shoemakers, and tailors alone made up nearly one third of the total Chinese labor force in San Francisco.[19] At that moment, the Chinese seemed to have an opportunity to be integrated into the mainstream economy. Unfortunately, their industry and frugality soon made them the target of racist hatred. As discussed in the introduction, this animus triggered a pattern of anti-Chinese violence throughout the western states. In the face of racial hostility, Chinese immigrants began in the 1880s to disperse to other parts of the country.[20] Some went to New York, where they hoped to find more racial tolerance than in California (but as the following chapters will tell us, they were treated only slightly better on the East Coast). By 1890, New York City was home to 2,048 Chinese and a Chinatown bordered by three streets in lower Manhattan—Mott, Pell, and Doyers—was recognizable.[21]

Early Chinese migration to the United States drew from a few regions, not the whole, of China. The bulk of emigrants to the United States came from three districts in Guangdong: San Yi (the Three-County District), Si Yi (the Four-County District), and Zhongshan. The three counties of San Yi are Panyu,

Shunde, and Nanhai; Si Yi consists of Taishan, Kaiping, Xinhui, and Enping; and Zhongshan is a county by itself (see maps 2.1 and 2.2). The location of these eight counties—close to the provincial capital Guangzhou—was an important reason why Chinese emigration to the United States originated in this area. For most of the time since the Tang Dynasty (618-907), Guangzhou (sometimes together with Quanzhou in southern Fujian Province) had been the only port in China opened to foreign merchants. People in Guangzhou and its environs had a longer tradition of receiving foreign merchants and were more familiar with seafaring than were China's inland residents. The deterioration of livelihood in Guangdong from the start of the nineteenth century was a powerful catalyst for many to cross the Pacific.

During the first half of the nineteenth century, Guangdong experienced numerous natural disasters, family feuds, rebellions, and government campaigns to smash rebellions. Decay was already under way when Emperor Qian Long (who reigned from 1736 to 1795) died in 1799. One of the most visible symptoms of the sickening dynasty was corruption of its officials.[22] Money for the improvement of agricultural production, for example, was embezzled by the rapacious Mandarins, leaving the dikes and dams in disrepair. As a result, floods became more frequent than previously.[23] And we should understand the consequences of these disasters in the context of explosive population growth during the second half of the eighteenth century: Between 1741 and 1800, China's population increased from 143 million to 300 million.[24] Life for many and especially for peasants was bleak. But despite the sufferings of the populace, the government demonstrated no intention to reduce taxes. On the contrary, taxes and levies became heavier and heavier as the ruling class sought to maintain their luxurious lives. It was only a matter of time before rebellions erupted.

The anger toward the exactions of tax collectors provoked the first major peasant revolt during the Qing dynasty, the White Lotus Rebellion, in 1796. By addressing the sufferings of poor peasants and by promising that the Maitreya Buddha would soon descend to the world to save them, the rebellion spread quickly in the border area where Shaanxi, Sichuan, and Hubei meet. It took Emperor Jia Qing (Qian Long's successor who reigned from 1796-1820) eight years to quell the revolt.[25] But what dealt the Qing dynasty a fatal blow was the Taiping Rebellion (the Heavenly Kingdom of Great Peace) of the mid-nineteenth century. The top leader of the rebellion, Hong Xiu Quan, was a Hakka school teacher who repeatedly failed to pass the civil service examinations. Hong later read some Christian missionary publications that he picked up in Guangzhou. Certain passages of the Old Testament probably echoed and exacerbated his anger with the Manchu rule. Hong soon organized the God-Worshippers' Society and declared himself the younger brother of Jesus Christ. Within a short time, the society mustered thousands of followers under Hong's leadership. The rebels initiated their cause in Guangxi in 1851 and eventually occupied the important provinces in south China for more than ten years. Although, with the help of Western powers, the Qing government finally suppressed the Taipings, the costs were huge: Vast farm lands were destroyed and 25 million people perished altogether. More importantly, the Heavenly Kingdom set in motion a series of local revolts that wreaked even greater havoc in Guangdong than had the Taiping Rebellion itself.

In the summer of 1850, rebels from Guangxi began raiding Guangdong. Before long, fifty thousand desperadoes took control of the city of Qingyuan, to the north of Guangzhou. Other secret societies, encouraged by this early victory, rose in Conghua in 1851. Within a year, a group of Taiping adherents captured Luoding, to the west of the capital city.[26] The year 1854 saw the uprisings of several peasant groups and secret societies near Guangzhou. Known as the Red Turbans because of the red headbands they wore, the rebels once seized the town of Foshan, just twenty miles from the capital city. Soon Guangzhou itself came under siege by the Red Turbans. The rebels' tactics of taxing only the rich unnerved the governor general who feared that the policy might attract more and more poor peasants to the Red Turbans' cause. In order to destroy cover for the outlaws, the banner troops set the entire northern suburbs on fire. Before the governor general finally brought the situation under control, a vast area in the province, including such emigrant counties as Xinhui, Kaiping, Panyu, Nanhai, and Shunde, had been devastated.[27]

While the rebels and government forces engaged each other in life-and-death struggles, Guangdong was being overrun by clan feuds. Wars between rival lineages often began with disputes over water rights and lands. In Huangpu, for example, two belligerent clans engaged each other in bloody battles for almost two full years, from 1835 to 1836.[28] But the picture of chaos would remain incomplete without mentioning the Bendi-Kejia war. The Bendi people, or Cantonese, were a group of Chinese who migrated to Guangdong from north China during the Tang dynasty. The Kejias, or guest families, represented Chinese who came to the province mainly during the late Song (960-1279). For centuries, the Kejias managed to keep their own tradition and, to the chagrin of the Bendis, occupied more and more farm land. Enmity toward the Kejias gradually built up. In the early years tensions between the two groups were under control. Violence eventually erupted in the mid-nineteenth century when the Kejias began cultivating land along the coast that the Qing government had forced the Bendis to evacuate in the seventeenth century to cut off potential support for the Ming loyalists. The Bendi-Kejia war, mainly waged in the Si Yi area, lasted for fourteen years and took a heavy toll of hundreds of lives.[29]

Internal and external crises, in fact, were haunting Guangdong simultaneously. An armed conflict between China and Britain, commonly known as the Opium War (1840-1842) exacerbated Cantonese peasants' poverty. For a long time in the eighteenth century, the trade between China and Britain was monopolized by the British East India Company. British merchants sold manufactured goods to the Chinese while purchasing tea, silk, porcelain, and other commodities from the Middle Kingdom. By the late eighteenth century, however, the company found itself in a trade deficit with China. To ameliorate the situation, the British began to smuggle opium, which they grew in India, into China. The Sino-British trade eventually balanced out at China's expense: Large amounts of silver flowed out of the Middle Kingdom while thousands of Chinese (especially in Guangdong) became addicted to opium. Alarmed by the deteriorating condition in Guangdong, the court sent Imperial Commissioner Lin Ze Xu to redress the problem. What followed was that Commissioner Lin ordered the destruction of the opium possessed by British merchants and the tightening of border controls to prevent further smuggling of opium into China. These moves led the British government to declare war on China. Britain started the Opium War for two purposes: to force China to open its doors to more trade and to punish the Middle Kingdom for the destruction of opium confiscated from British merchants. China lost the war and was forced to sign the Treaty of Nanjing, an unequal treaty, with the British in 1842. This compelled China to open five ports (Guangzhou, Xiamen, Fuzhou, Ningpo, and Shanghai) to British merchants, to grant foreigners extraterritoriality, to cede Hong Kong, and to pay Britain a heavy indemnity (21 million Spanish silver dollars).

Other Western powers quickly followed suit. Taking advantage of China's weakness, the United States signed the Treaty of Wangxia with China in 1844, and France signed the Treaty of Huangpu in the same year. In the late 1850s, a second Opium War broke out, which resulted in the signing of the Treaty of Tianjin (1860). The new pact granted Western powers, Britain, France, Russia, and the United States, more commercial privileges and indemnities. More ports, many in inland China, were opened, the ban on the opium trade was lifted, and foreign missionaries got more freedom and protection from the Chinese government.[30] The Opium Wars and the unequal treaties affected the San Yi and Si Yi areas more than others. Inhabitants of these counties suffered, for example, from the increased taxes arising from the indemnities. The increased import of consumer goods after the war also seriously hurt the peasants' household industry.[31] Understandably, those who outlived the wars and disasters began looking for new chances for survival. These counties' proximity to Hong Kong and Macao enabled their residents to learn about overseas opportunities quickly. Desperate to improve their lives, some impoverished peasants became restless on hearing that earning money was easy in the United States.

Though San Yi and Si Yi alike were emigrant districts, they differed in the numbers of people who left them for the United States. Table 2.1 illustrates that immigrants from Si Yi far outnumbered those from San Yi. More immigrants to New York, as well as California, came from Si Yi than those from San Yi.[32] Although the majority of Chinese immigrants in America originated from Si Yi, the San Yi people, especially merchants and artisans, came to the United States first. The early San Francisco Chinatown merchants, for example, originated

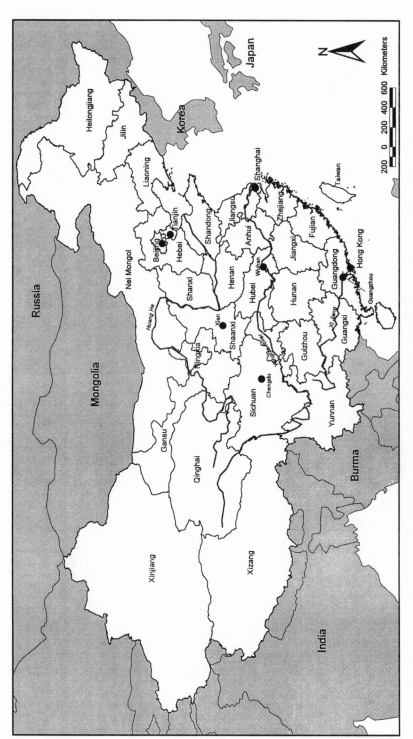

Map 2.1. China. Before 1950, the overwhelming majority of Chinese immigrants to the United States originated from Guangdong Province.

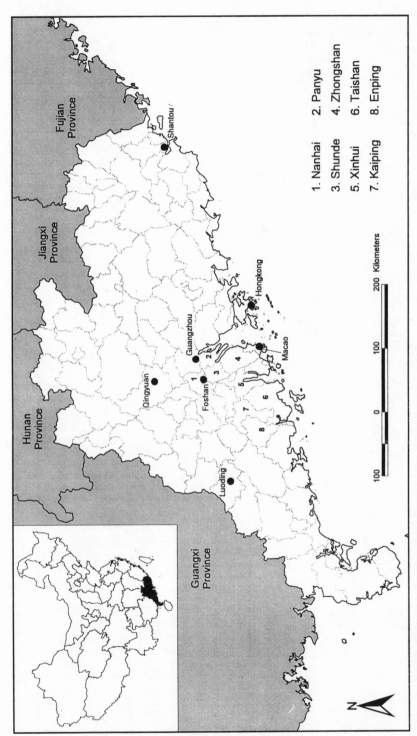

Map 2.2. Guangdong Province and Locations of Eight Emigrant Counties

1. Nanhai
2. Panyu
3. Shunde
4. Zhongshan
5. Xinhui
6. Taishan
7. Kaiping
8. Enping

Fujian Province

Jiangxi Province

Hunan Province

Guangxi Province

Shantou

Qingyuan

Guangzhou

Foshan

Hongkong

Macao

Luoding

200 Kilometers

100

0

100

N

mostly from San Yi. Chinese artisans who came to California in the early 1850s, including those who built the Parrot Building at the corner of California and Montgomery Streets, were also mostly from San Yi.[33] As we shall see in chapter 3, San Yi had a diversified economy. This meant a large number of people who were not peasants or even farmers lived in San Yi. This absence of ties to agriculture was probably an important reason for the earlier emigration of San Yi people, especially the artisans. Closeness to Guangzhou provided the San Yi residents with the chance to learn a trade or engage in small businesses there. Concomitantly, it allowed them to become better informed of overseas opportunities. Mobility and urban experience probably made the San Yi merchants and artisans more ready to migrate than did the rural lives of the Si Yi peasants.

Interestingly, the early Chinese immigrants who arrived in New York in the 1860s, 1850s, or even earlier had a strong tendency to adopt Anglo American names, marry European American women, and become U.S. citizens. The proportion of the early New York Chinese visiting the Fourth Avenue Presbyterian Church was also notably high.[34] John Huston, possibly the first New York Chinese to be naturalized, was born in China and brought to New York at the age of two. He married an Irish woman and settled down in Manhattan.[35] Many early Chinese settlers in New York were sailors and skilled workers with urban experience, often from living in Hong Kong or Macao before migrating to the United States.[36] According to a *New York Tribune* report in 1885, one of the first Chinese to settle in New York was Ah Sue, a cook and steward working for a packet ship. Tired of seafaring, he opened a tobacco and candy store at No. 62 Cherry Street in 1847 and married an Irish woman the following year.[37] Appo, another Chinese, who owned a tea store on Spring

Table 2.1. Chinese in California by District Origin

District Origin	1855		1866		1868	
	No.	%	No.	%	No.	%
Si Yi	16,107	41.6	32,500	55.8	35,900	58.8
Zhongshan	14,000	36.2	11,500	19.7	11,800	19.4
San Yi	6,800	17.6	10,500	18.0	10,000	16.4
Kejias	1,780	4.6	3,800	6.5	3,300	5.4

	1876		ca 1926-1928		1950	
	No.	%	No.	%	No.	%
Si Yi	124,000	82.0	23,000	82.5	37,000	74.0
Zhongshan	12,000	7.9	2,500	9.5	7,000	14.0
San Yi	11,000	7.3	1,500	6.0	5,000	10.0
Kejias	4,300	2.8	500	2.0	1,000	2.0

Source: Thomas W. Chinn, *A History of the Chinese in California: A Syllabus* (San Francisco: Chinese Historical Society of America, 1969), 20.

Street in the 1850s, married an English woman. Appo's friends expressed their intention of learning to read and write English, becoming U.S. citizens, and marrying American women.[38]

In the late 1860s, New York City claimed one hundred Chinese residents. Half of them were cigarmakers, the other half were cigar vendors or sailors. The New York Chinese at this time obviously wanted to develop roots in America and were indeed doing so. About fifty of them had Irish or German wives.[39] Hong Kee Kang, a former sailor and later a cigarmaker at 500 Pearl Street, had served in the navy as a steward during the American Civil War, supplying powder for the guns on the gunboat *Albatross*. He received an honorable discharge in 1864.[40] Ah Woh, another cigarmaker living on Baxter Street, was naturalized in 1863. He had probably also volunteered military service during the Civil War.[41] By the early 1870s, the New York Chinese population had increased to five hundred and cigar making remained one of the major occupations for them.[42]

The relatively handsome income from making cigars was probably the motivation for these Chinese to settle down in New York instead of returning to China. A Chinese cigarmaker reportedly earned as much as $100 a month in the 1860s.[43] Contrary to the stereotype that Chinese immigrants undercut native workers' wages, Chinese cigarmakers working on Maiden Lane in New York City in the 1880s demanded $15 to $16 per thousand cigars during their strikes while their German counterparts only took $8 to $9.[44]

These cigarmakers clearly represented a group of artisans. An artisan, according to H. Mayhew, "is an educated handicraftsman, following a calling that requires an apprenticeship of greater or lesser duration whereas a labourer's occupation needs no education whatsoever."[45] During most of the nineteenth century, when cigars were made by hand, it took at least nine months' apprenticeship to learn the trade. For a long time in American as well as in western European history, possession of special skills enabled artisans to exercise substantial control over their workplaces, including such important matters as working hours, output, and the training of apprentices.[46] This autonomy, however, was gradually encroached upon by the advent of modern capitalism, which transformed artisans into workers. Both the revolution in the market, expressed in the pressure to lower prices, and the one in technology, expressed in mechanization and the factory system, threatened artisans with the danger of extinction. Understandably, artisans put up strong resistance to the impact of capitalism and became the forerunners of the labor movement.[47] Trade unionism—demands for higher wages and lower hours—championed by the skilled craftsmen had remained a dominant theme in the American labor movement for more than one hundred years. By the late nineteenth century, the introduction of machines such as cigar molds and the new technology of streamlining had revolutionized cigar production in cities on the eastern seaboard. In New York City, entrepreneurs also broke down the production of

Table 2.2. Immigration to the United States from Northern and Southern Italy, 1899-1910

Year	Number		Percent	
	North Italy	South Italy	North Italy	South Italy
1899	11,821	65,587	15.3	84.7
1900	15,799	84,329	15.8	84.2
1901	20,324	115,659	14.9	85.1
1902	25,485	152,883	14.3	85.7
1903	34,571	195,993	15.0	85.0
1904	34,056	159,127	17.6	82.4
1905	35,802	185,445	16.2	83.8
1906	40,940	231,921	15.0	85.0
1907	47,814	237,680	16.7	83.3
1908	21,494	106,824	16.7	83.1
1909	22,220	160,800	12.1	87.9
1910	26,699	188,616	12.4	87.6

Source: Reports of the Immigration Commission, Vol. 4, Immigration Conditions in Europe (Washington, D.C., 1911), 141.

cigars into simpler tasks. This enabled employers to hire more and more women to do the job.[48] As their mainstream counterparts had, Chinese cigarmakers must also have felt the threat of extinction. As we shall see in chapter 6, Chinese cigarmakers in New York demonstrated tremendous radicalism in the 1880s.

It is not clear that all these early Chinese settlers were from San Yi. The fact that most early Chinese immigrants in California hailed from San Yi suggests this is the case.[49] Chinese artisans, then, appear in a vanguard in crossing the Pacific and becoming settled in New York. After the 1880s, peasant immigrants began to arrive in New York in large groups and quickly outnumbered the artisans. As the discussion of chapter 3 shows, these peasant immigrants intended to return to their home villages in Guangdong after a period in America. There is a clear contrast between them and the artisans who intended to settle down in New York.

Just as few Chinese migrated to New York City before the 1880s, so, too, was the number of Italians who lived there before that decade. In 1880, only 12,223 Italians, mainly from northern and central Italy, resided in New York.[50] Among these early Italian immigrants were musicians, peddlers, workers, and political emigrés. In the 1880s, special conditions in Italy (which we shall discuss shortly) prompted large waves of Italians, mainly from the rural areas in southern Italy and Sicily, to cross the Atlantic Ocean to the United States. By the 1890s immigrants from the *mezzogiorno* had far outnumbered those from northern Italy.[51] Table 2.2 clearly illustrates the situation.

As with Chinese emigration, this new wave of immigrants hailed only from several selected areas in the *mezzogiorno*, especially Calabria, Abruzzi, Basilicata, and western Sicily (Map 2.3). New York, which offered more employment opportunities than other cities, always received the most Italian immigrants. A careful study of the passports issued to the potential emigrants in a Sicilian town in 1901 indicates that New York was chosen by 30 percent of the applicants as their final destination.[52] So many of them chose to settle in New York that by the year 1890 the Italian population in this city had reached 94,915.[53] According to a report in *Harper's Weekly* in 1890, several Little Italys had already appeared in the city: one in East Harlem around 115th Street, one in the western section of Greenwich Village, and another along Mulberry Street.[54] As time went by, Little Italys emerged in the New York boroughs of Brooklyn, Queens, and Staten Island.[55]

In another parallel with Chinese emigration that started in San Yi but later involved more people in Si Yi, the earliest Italian immigrants did not originate from rural southern Italy or Sicily from where most Italian immigrants ultimately came, but from northern Italy. In northern Italy, especially the Genoa area, earlier industrialization made residents more mobile than their southern compatriots. Accustomed to competition and mobility, a great proportion of northern Italian workmen were inclined to migrate; indeed, emigration from north Italy to the neighboring European countries had commenced as early as the sixteenth century. These northern emigrants included, along with peasants, masons, stonecutters, blacksmiths, furnace workers, and carpenters.[56] Not surprisingly, when in the nineteenth century came the news that America was a land of plenty, these northerners and especially artisans from there were the first to leave.

Chinese and Italian emigration patterns do not wholly match, however. An important motivation for the southern Italians to leave their native villages and try their luck overseas was poverty exacerbated by the development of capitalism in Italy and the involvement of southern Italy's economy in the world market. The unification movement (*Risorgimento*) gave a tremendous impetus to the development of the Italian economy. It hastened the accumulation of capital, made possible the construction of nationwide transportation systems, and facilitated domestic as well as international commerce. But these developments often occurred at the expense of the south.[57] Protective tariffs, for example, aimed at safeguarding the industries in the north. As a result, the underdeveloped southern industries were in an inferior position to their northern counterparts. Many southern factories went bankrupt and large numbers of workers became unemployed.[58] The situation for the agricultural population was even worse.

During the last quarter of the nineteenth century, the price of wheat in the world market continuously fell, and Italy's wheat imports often exceeded its exports. Moreover, with the cultivation of citrus orchards in California and Florida, the United States reduced its imports of oranges and lemons from Italy.

Map 2.3. Italy and Its Emigrant Regions.

Consequently, citrus farmers in Calabria, Basilicata, and Sicily suffered heavy losses. At the same time, France adopted many protective measures against the import of Italian wines, which forced many grape farmers in Apulia, Calabria, and Sicily into bankruptcy.[59] But southern Italian peasants did not seem to be— in fact many of them were not—fatalists, because they always wished to improve the quality of their lives. Once aware that the opportunity to improve their lot at home was slim, the peasants, or the *contadini*, turned their eyes to the United States, the land of plenty.

The capitalist transformation in Europe, therefore, was the chief reason for nineteenth century European emigration. This was clearly so for Italian emigration. In emphasizing the effect of capitalism on emigration, the historian John Bodnar has written that "most of the [European] immigrants transplanted to America in the century of industrial growth after 1830 were in reality the children of capitalism."[60] One expression of this capitalist influence was that Italian immigrants included many artisans and craftsmen, who later would become leaders in the Italian labor movement in New York. Italian artisans already had abundant experience in the market-oriented economy, trade unionism, and political elections before they emigrated. Experience with capitalism was not confined to artisans alone; by the nineteenth century, many southern Italian peasants had also become familiar with this new way of life. The meager income from individual small parcels of land was hardly enough to support the families who worked them. As a result, many peasants had to sell their labor as farm workers to the landlords to keep body and soul together.[61] By becoming wage earners—albeit in most cases it was only part time—many *contadini* took an important, though still rudimentary, lesson in capitalism, the wage-labor system. Also accompanying the development of the capitalist economy was a kind of proto-labor activism: Some Italian peasants became involved in agricultural strikes and were exposed to ideas such as trade unionism and socialism.

The development of capitalism influenced emigration from Guangdong as well as from Italy, although its influence differed in the two places. The Opium Wars led to examples of exogenous capitalism in Guangdong that had no parallel in Italy. Capitalism in Guangdong was, on the whole, less developed than in Italy during the same period of the century. It is true, however, that, by the nineteenth century, agriculture in some areas of Guangdong had undergone a certain degree of commercialization, one dimension of capitalism. While in Italy and most other European countries, the emergence of capitalist agriculture was accompanied by the transformation of tenants into wage-earning farm laborers, even by the 1930s, the majority of the agricultural population in the emigrant communities in Guangdong were still considered tenants (see table 2.3).

Though perhaps inconclusive, these figures do strongly suggest that tenants far outnumbered wage-earning laborers in the areas from which the bulk of Chinese emigrants came to the United States. Capitalism had not yet crucially

Table 2.3. Percentage of Wage-Earning Laborers in Si Yi, San Yi, and Zhongshan, 1936

County	Number of Families	Number of Tenants	% of Tenants	Wage Laborers	% of Laborers
Shunde	3,150	1,983	63.0	300	9.5
Panyu	26,971	16,043	59.5	2,204	8.2
Zhongshan	1,875	1,009	53.8	61	3.3
Taishan	1,224	737	60.2	63	5.1
Kaiping	224	80	35.7	5	2.2

Source: Han-sheng Chen, *Landlord and Peasant in China: A Study of the Agrarian Crisis in South China* (New York: International Publishers, 1936), 115-21.

changed everyday relations and values in village life. In spite of the fact that the aftermath of the Opium Wars in a way did speed up the process of Chinese emigration, this exogenous capitalism was only limited to some coastal cities. Thus, traditional lineage solidarity still characterized typical landlord-tenant relationship in Guangdong.

Table 2.4 illustrates another difference between Chinese and Italian immigration. Among Chinese immigrants, the number of artisans, skilled workers, and professionals was far smaller than among Italian immigrants. Why so few Chinese artisans became immigrants is unclear. If the capitalist transformation in Guangdong had been complete, or at least as extensive as the one in southern Italy, then there should have been a large number of artisans thrown out of their old trades. Given the facts that San Yi and Si Yi were so close to Guangzhou and Hong Kong, and that artisans were unattached to the land, it is hard to imagine that the handicraftsmen would not join the peasants in migrating to the land of plenty.

In migrating to the United States, both Italian and Chinese peasants were entering a thoroughly capitalist society, although they may not have been aware of this fact. Once arrived, their experience of capitalist development at home would naturally affect their adjustment to American society. For example, and especially, the attitudes they held toward trade unions would make this adjustment either easy or difficult. As Bodnar points out, "The [European] immigrant did not encounter capitalism for the first time in American cities; he had already encountered some of its manifestations prior to departing and had arrived at certain decisions of how it should be encountered."[62] Italians migrated from an embryonic to a full-fledged capitalist society. The Chinese peasants' migration, on the other hand, was a more abrupt change to a far less familiar, indeed almost wholly unknown, environment. The wage-labor system, class consciousness, and trade unionism were all unfamiliar to these immigrants from East Asia.

Table 2.4. Occupational Experience of Italian and Chinese Immigrants Arriving in the United States during 1901-1910

	Italian			Chinese		
Year	Profes-sionals	Skilled workmen	% of total immigrants	Profes-sionals	Skilled workmen	% of total immigrants
1901	505	17,319	12.93	16	54	2.85
1902	484	20,730	11.75	3	2	0.36
1903	727	31,661	13.87	2	12	0.64
1904	1,114	30,655	16.21	21	42	1.46
1905	1,059	27,897	12.79	28	75	5.23
1906	1,253	37,561	13.52	9	19	1.89
1907	1,038	34,518	12.09	3	1	0.52
1908	784	16,671	12.91	31	0	2.45
1909	460	13,428	7.29	13	4	0.92
1910	690	20,028	9.27	19	4	1.30

Source: Annual Report of the Immigration Commission, 1901-1910. For the category of professionals, this table does not include, as the commission's report did, governmental officials; nor does this table include non-specified professionals, which is dubious.

Notes

1. Pei Chi Liu, *Mei Guo Hua Qiao Shi (A History of the Chinese in the United States of America)* (Taipei: Li Ming Wen Hua Shi Ye Gu Fen You Xian Gong Si, 1976), 9-15; Jack Chen: *The Chinese of America: From the Beginnings to the Present* (San Francisco: Harper & Row Publishers, 1981), 5-6.

2. Chen, *The Chinese of America*, 6.

3. Takaki, *Strangers from a Different Shore*, 80-81.

4. Loren W. Fessler, *Chinese in America: Stereotyped Past, Changing Present* (New York: Vantage Press, 1983), 9, 11, 239.

5. Tchen, *New York Before Chinatown*, 41-96.

6. United States Government, U.S. Bureau of the Census, *The Tenth Census, 1880,* Vol. I, *Population* (Washington, D.C.: Government Printing House, 1883), 422.

7. United States Government, U.S. Bureau of the Census, *The Tenth Census, 1880,* Vol. I, *Population,* 379.

8. Chen, *The Chinese of America*, 66-67.

9. John Blum, William S. McFeely, Edmund S. Morgan, Arthur M. Schlesinger, Jr., Kenneth M. Stampp, and C. Vann Woodward, *The National Experience: A History of the United States* (Fort Worth, Tex.: Harcourt Brace Jovanovich, 1993), 411.

10. Saxton, *The Indispensable Enemy*, 62.

11. Chan, *Asian Americans*, 30-31.

12. Chen, *The Chinese of America*, 68.

13. Cited in Chen, *The Chinese of America*, 68.

14. Saxton, *The Indispensable Enemy*, 62, 65.

15. When the Qing (1644-1911) replaced the Ming Dynasty (1368-1644), many Ming loyalists, especially members of the Triad Society, fled to southeast Asia where they established some anti-Qing strongholds in hopes of returning to China someday to drive the Manchus out. In order to cut off the connection between the Ming loyalists in southeast Asia and their potential supporters in China proper, the Qing government felt it necessary to prohibit the Chinese from going abroad. The death penalty would be imposed on those who dared to leave the country. The ban on overseas migration was not lifted until the late nineteenth century.

16. Sucheng Chan, *This Bittersweet Soil: The Chinese in California Agriculture, 1860-1910* (Berkeley: University of California Press, 1986), 37.

17. There were 105,465 Chinese immigrants in the United States in 1880. See United States Government, U.S. Bureau of the Census, *The Tenth Census, 1880*, Vol. I, *Population*, 379.

18. Ping Chiu, *Chinese Labor in California, 1850-1880: An Economic Study* (Madison, Wisc.: The State Historical Society of Wisconsin, for the Department of History, the University of Wisconsin, Madison, 1963), 65.

19. John W. Stephens, "A Quantitative History of Chinatown, San Francisco, 1870 and 1880," in *The Life, Influence and Role of the Chinese in the United States, 1776-1960*, Proceedings/Papers of the National Conference held at the University of San Francisco, 1975 (San Francisco: The Chinese Historical Society of America, 1976), 78.

20. *New York Times*, 7 May 1880.

21. United States Government, Bureau of the Census, *The Eleventh Census, 1890*, Vol. I, *Population* (Washington, D.C.: Government Printing House, 1895), 646.

22. He Shen (1750-1799), Emperor Qian Long's most favored courtier, presented an extreme case of this widespread corruption. He began as the emperor's bodyguard at the age of twenty-five and within a few years moved up to the rank of grand councilor. He held almost twenty different posts in the government, which provided him with the best opportunity to rob the state treasury. By the time he was arrested and indicted upon the sovereign's death, He had allegedly accumulated a fortune worth $1.5 billion. See John King Fairbank and Edwin O. Reischauer, *China: Tradition and Transformation* (Boston: Houghton Mifflin Company, 1989), 239-40; and Chen, *The Chinese of America*, 7.

23. During its 267-year history, the Qing Dynasty experienced 282 natural disasters, an average of more than one per year.

24. Chen, *The Chinese of America*, 7.

25. John King Fairbank, *China: A New History* (Cambridge, Mass.: The Belknap Press of Harvard University Press, 1994), 189-90.

26. Frederick Wakeman, Jr., *Strangers at the Gate: Social Disorder in South China, 1839-1861* (Berkeley: University of California Press, 1966), 132-33.

27. Wakeman, *Strangers at the Gate*, 139-48.

28. Wakeman, *Strangers at the Gate*, 112.

29. Chen, *The Chinese of America*, 9.

30. Chan, *This Bittersweet Soil*, 22-23; *Ding Yi Li, Zhong Mei Zao Qi Wai Jiao Shi, 1784-1894 (A History of the Early Diplomatic Relations between China and the United States, 1784-1894)* (Taipei: San Min Shu Ju, 1985), 348-49.

31. Chan, *This Bittersweet Soil*, 20, 22-23. See also Chan, "European and Asian Immigration into the United States in Comparative Perspectives, 1820s to 1920s," in

Immigration Reconsidered, ed. Yangs-McLaughlin, 42-44.

32. Betty Lee Sung, *Mountain of Gold: The Story of the Chinese in America* (New York: MacMillian, 1967), 13.

33. Chan, *This Bittersweet Soil*, 29; see also Chan, "European and Asian Immigration into the United States in Comparative Perspective, 1820s to 1920s," in *Immigration Reconsidered*, ed. Yans-McLaughlin, 44.

34. *New York Times*, 30 May 1869. For intermarriage between Chinese immigrants and white women, see Wong Chin Foo, "The Chinese in New York," *Cosmopolitan*, Vol. 5, No. 4 (June 1888), 308; also see John Kuo Wei Tchen, "New York Chinese: The Nineteenth-Century Pre-Chinatown Settlement," *Chinese America: History and Perspectives* (January 1990), 161-65.

35. Tchen, *New York Before Chinatown*, 76.

36. *New York Times*, 26 December 1856 and 30 May 1869.

37. *New York Tribune*, 21 June 1885.

38. *New York Times*, 26 December 1856.

39. *New York Times*, 30 May 1869.

40. *New York Tribune*, 17 August and 28 September 1904, cited in Arthur Bonner, *Alas!* 17.

41. Bonner, *Alas!* 17.

42. Tchen, "New York Chinese," *Chinese America* (January 1990), 168.

43. *New York Times*, 30 May 1869.

44. Bonner, *Alas!* 42.

45. H. Mayhew, *The Morning Chronicle Survey*, Vol. 3 (Faliban, Firle, 1981), 189, cited in David Green, *From Artisans to Paupers: Economic Change and Poverty in London, 1790-1870* (Aldershot, Hants, England: Scholar Press, 1995), 87.

46. Thomas Max Safley and Leonard N. Rosenband, "Introduction," in Thomas Max Safley and Leonard N. Rosenband eds. *The Workplace before the Factory: Artisans and Proletarians, 1500-1800* (Ithaca, N.Y.: Cornell University Press, 1993), 4.

47. Bruce Laurie, *Artisans into Workers: Labor in Nineteenth-Century America* (New York: Hill and Wang, 1989), 15-73.

48. Tchen, "New York Chinese," 173.

49. A study of the 1880 San Francisco Chinatown shows that Chinese sailors of San Yi origin made up 2.1 percent of the residents while the Si Yi sailors made up only 0.4 percent. The situation in the early New York Chinatown must not be very different from this picture. See John W. Stephens, "A Quantitative History of Chinatown, San Francisco, 1870 and 1880," 84. Some of these cigarmakers probably learned the skills for making cigars in Cuba when they were released from the plantations, and then re-migrated to New York City. See Tchen, *New York Before Chinatown*, 227; Bonner, Alas! 18.

50. United States Government, U.S. Bureau of the Census, *The Tenth Census, 1880*, Vol. I, *Population*, 521.

51. *Reports of the Immigration Commission*, Vol. 4, *Emigration Conditions in Europe* (Washington, D.C., 1911), 141.

52. John W. Briggs, *An Italian Passage: Immigrants to Three American Cities, 1890-1930* (New Haven, Conn.: Yale University Press, 1978), 70-71.

53. United States Government, Bureau of the Census, *The Eleventh Census, 1890*,

Vol. I, *Population*, clxix and 672.

54. *Harper's Weekly*, 18 October 1890.

55. For the establishment of new Little Italys in the various boroughs of New York at the turn of the century, see *New York Tribune*, 20 August 1901.

56. Robert E. Foerster, *The Italian Emigration of Our Times* (Cambridge, Mass.: Harvard University Press, 1924), 122-23.

57. Shepard B. Clough, *The Economic History of Modern Italy* (New York: Columbia University Press, 1964), 66-67, 111-12.

58. Humbert S. Nelli, *From Immigrants to Ethnics: The Italian Americans* (New York: Oxford University Press, 1983), 22-23. See also Christopher Seton-Watson, *Italy from Liberalism to Fascism, 1870-1925* (Frome: Methuen, 1967), 21-22.

59. Clough, *The Economic History of Modern Italy*, 117, 120-21. Alexander DeConde, *Half Bitter, Half Sweet, An Excursion into Italian-American History* (New York: Scribner, 1971), 79.

60. John Bodnar, *The Transplanted: A History of Immigrants in Urban America* (Bloomington, Ind.: Indiana University Press, 1985), 1.

61. William E. Davenport, "The Exodus of a Latin People," in *The Italians, Social Backgrounds of an American Group*, ed. Francesco Cordasco and Eugene Bucchioni (Clifton, N.J.: A.M. Kelley, 1974), 98.

62. Bodnar, *The Transplanted*, 54.

3

Returning Home or Staying in America?

The problem of the immigrants' return migration deserves special attention. For a long time, references to the Chinese as sojourners in America and to the Europeans as immigrants indicated that scholars failed to place Chinese and European immigration on an equal footing.[1] Moreover, the argument that Chinese immigrants' intention to return home provoked the anti-Chinese movement is tantamount to ascribing to the Chinese themselves the responsibility for their mistreatment.[2] Since the 1960s, some researchers have attempted to correct this imbalance. When deploring the fact that "Asians were somehow outside the canon of immigration history," Roger Daniels pointed out in the mid-1960s that "it seems much more reasonable to make the opposite assumption: that immigrants from Asia were, first of all, immigrants, and that, until uncontrovertible evidence to the contrary is offered, the generalizations which apply to most immigrants also apply to Asians."[3]

In the 1980s, Franklin Ng also questioned historians' separating Chinese from European immigration. Citing important findings in European immigration, Ng contended that like many Chinese who intended to return to China, so, too, did large numbers of Europeans. In their sojourner mentality and the preservation of ethnic cultures, Chinese and European immigrants showed comparable patterns and should be treated as equals.[4] In her recent article "European and Asian Immigration into the United States in Comparative Perspective, 1820s to 1920s," Sucheng Chan went even further by suggesting that the desire to purchase land at home motivated both European and Asian peasants to migrate to the United States. Because of this motivation, landholding situations at home largely determined patterns of European and Asian emigration: Most immigrants came from areas where land was widely distributed and available for sale.[5] The balance of this chapter uses the history of Chinese immigrants in New York to test the validity of the theses of Daniels, Ng, and Chan. We shall also address the important question of why, in the early 1950s, Chinese immigrants abruptly dropped their sojourner mentality and decided to stay in the United States.

I

A salient feature of early Chinese immigration to the United States lay in its continued return migration: Like their brethren in other American cities, Chinese immigrants who had chosen New York as their second home did not intend to stay in the New World permanently. Their goal was to accumulate wealth through hard work and thrift, and then to return to their native villages to lead a comfortable life. Louis J. Beck, a journalist who wrote an account of the New York Chinese community of the 1890s, reported that the Chinese in New York were "mere birds of passage . . . whose business relations here are at best but temporary."[6] The tendency of Chinese immigrants to return home was reflected in the fact that New York City's Chinese population lacked a significant elderly group before the 1950s. Table 3.1 illustrates the pattern.

The table indicates that most New York Chinese returned to China after retirement.[7] Even as late as 1945, most Chinese immigrants in New York still wished to return to China once the war with Japan was over. To persuade them to remain, *Min Qi Ri Bao (The Chinese Nationalist Daily)*, a Chinese-language newspaper published by the pro-Kuomintang[8] immigrants in New York, drafted a special editorial in 1945 that read:

> According to recent developments in our Chinese immigrant community, the general public's view is that, after the victory over Japan, all Chinese immigrants will return to our country instead of staying in this ludicrous foreign land. There are three reasons for this: the abhorrence of a wandering life, the willingness to contribute to the construction of the motherland, and the reluctance to endure foreigners' discrimination. . . . But, if viewed from another angle, this idea [of returning home] is selfish and indifferent to what the situation requires of us. We are against the return home of all Chinese immigrants and are especially opposed to the return of those who are knowledgeable about Chinese immigrant communities. We hope that the history of Chinese immigrant communities, which has been written with blood and tears, shall not perish.

The editorial went on to console the immigrants:

> We could go to China once in a while to visit our motherland and hometown. In this way, we may feel better and be wholehearted in improving our Chinese immigrant communities. We could also bring family members back and develop roots here. . . . After the war, we are sure, the advance in science will make it very convenient to travel between the two antipodes [*sic*].[9]

For many decades, Chinese immigrants in New York were concerned primarily with the latest happenings in China, especially in their hometowns, rather than

Table 3.1. Percentage of Age Distribution of Chinese Population in New York City by Sex, 1940

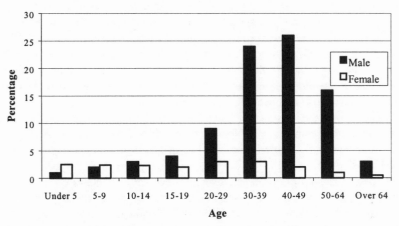

Source: United States Government, U.S. Bureau of the Census, *The Sixteenth Census, 1940*, Vol. I, *Population* (Washington, D.C.: Government Printing House, 1942).

with events in the United States.[10] Before the 1950s, with few exceptions, the front page as well as most other pages of a Chinese newspaper always carried news about China. On November 6, 1952, the New York Chinese newspaper *Mei Zhou Hua Qiao Ri Bao (China Daily News)* published the report on the election of President Dwight Eisenhower on the fifth page (it only had six pages in all), while the news on the front page was all about China.[11]

Like their Chinese counterparts, Italian immigrants were eager to return to their native villages. In the late 1880s when the wave of immigrants from southern Italy first began to swell New York City's Italian population, the tendency among these newcomers to return home had already caught public attention. As *Harper's Weekly* magazine observed in 1889:

> There are in and around New York about 85,000 Italian laborers of the lowest peasant class. Less than one-fourth of the adults are women. They came almost always with the intention of returning to Italy as soon as they shall have gathered enough out of the plenty of this country to suffice for their simple wants at home.[12]

In Greenwich Village, the turnover of the Italian population between 1910 and 1914 was 75 percent since the majority of these immigrants returned home after staying in New York for a few years.[13] A group of Sicilians, who had settled in the neighborhood of East 69th Street and Avenue A, also expected to return to their native villages in Cinici. Among them the frequently heard questions were: "I wonder if I can go back in time for the next crop?" and "I hope I can get back in time for the festa."[14] Once when planning the celebration of the festival of Santa Fara, the patron saint of Cinisi, many people objected that the money should be sent to Cinisi for the event there. After the festival was held in New York in April 1919, the Cinisians were so disappointed that their wish to return to Cinisi to see the original grew stronger. At the same time, the settlers kept their hometown informed on the latest developments in their settlement in New York. They reported to their fellow townsmen back in Cinici those who transgressed the old customs while in New York. They obviously feared for their reputation in Cinisi because most of them expected to go back.[15]

The homeland orientation of Italian immigrants also pervaded the newspapers they published in New York. Consider, for example, *Il Progresso Italo-Americano*, the most influential Italian-language daily in New York and the United States. During the 1890s, the newspaper had a special column, captioned *"Cronaca D'Italia,"* exclusively devoted to the news on Italy. By the early twentieth century, the news under *"Cronaca D'Italia"* was further classified into Calabria, Abruzzi, Sicilia, Basilicata, and so on.[16] These provinces sent the bulk of Italian immigrants to the United States. Not until the mid-1920s did the waves of immigration from Italy lose their back tow. As *United America*, a weekly magazine run by Italians in New York, observed in 1925:

> The work of helping aliens to obtain American citizenship is more impor-
> tant today than ever owning to the fact that the bulk of the immigrants are
> now coming to this country to stay, while most of the foreign born already
> here do not expect to return to Europe. Before the passage of immigration
> restriction laws our foreign population was less stable, many thousands
> staying here only long enough to earn sufficient money to retire or to live
> in comparative ease in their native land.[17]

Native-born New Yorkers quickly concluded that in their views on return migration Italian and Chinese immigrants were more similar than different. The *New York Tribune* expressed a concern arising from this view as early as 1895:

> America is such a huge and undeveloped land that it can stand a flood of
> immigration, provided only that the immigrants are hardy, laborious fel-
> lows, who ask no more than to become good citizens as fast as they can
> learn the language and get out naturalization papers. If, however, they
> came to underbid native labor and to save up their surplus cash only to go
> back home and live happily ever after in Italy or in China, the United
> States may well consider whether it has any use for them.[18]

The 1890s *Tribune* editors seemed unaware that the Chinese Exclusion Act had made it impossible for Chinese immigrants to take out naturalization papers.

II

More and more, recent studies of European immigration suggest that, although many factors in the New World, and especially discrimination against the newcomers, were responsible for continued return migration, these factors merely strengthened the immigrants' intention to return home. As we shall see shortly, before embarking for America, the emigrants had already made plans for eventually going back to their native villages.

Italian immigrants, as many recent studies show, were not simply pushed out of their homeland by poverty, although many of them were indeed poor. Instead, like many other immigrant groups, they actively sought improvement in their lives. Before leaving their native country, the *contadini* had set a major economic goal for themselves: to accumulate money abroad to purchase land at home. "It is not hard conditions or starvation that now send Italians to America," observed Adolfo Rossi, inspector of Italy's emigration department, "They come because they are eager for more money."[19] *Onore*—honor for one's family—had long occupied a central position in the value system of Italian peasants. By the late nineteenth century, as the capitalist transformation of agriculture made the Italian society increasingly competitive, the word *onore* gained a new dimension. Now a more meaningful way to obtain *onore* was to enhance one's economic status in the native village.[20] The Italian peasant was envious of those returned migrants who looked like *signori* and who could afford to buy land and houses. This envy was soon followed by his own decision for transoceanic migration.[21] The prospect of becoming small proprietors with "the assurance of a house and land and comfort for his family in his native *paese*" was the most important factor that encouraged the Italian to endure hardships abroad.[22] Italian emigrants sent money home to purchase land before they themselves returned. The Italian consul and many bankers in New York told a tourist in the 1890s that Italian immigrants in that city alone sent 25 to 27 million lira (more than U.S. $6 million) to Italy annually.[23] According to the supervisor of land sale in Consenza in southern Italy, in 1900, 90 percent of the land was purchased with money remitted from the United States.[24] The New York Italians' desire to return home and purchase land was so strong that they vigorously demanded representation in the Italian parliament. In persuading the parliament to give representation to these expatriates, a social worker for the Italians pointed out in 1906 that a great number of New York Italians had bought land at home.

> The fact that many Italians here return to their mother country and that an even greater number hold real property there and invest yearly, relatively large sums in farm lands at home, and the grounds for giving such expatriated Italians political representation in the home parliament becomes apparent. Indeed, it is quite probable that "Little Italy" in New York contributed more to the tax roll of Italy than some of the poorest provinces in

Sicily or Galabria.[25]

Italian peasants' attachment to land and their desire to become small landowners were well known. However, during the post-*Risorgimento* land reform, northern Italy, central Italy, and Apulia lacked a wide distribution of land.[26] The areas that really benefitted from the land reform and experienced broad distribution of property were the deep south and Sicily.[27] The initial purpose of the land reform was to create a large number of small farmers in order to give the national economy a boost. Though the land reform did not bring about a rapid economic growth as the policy makers had expected, the number of landholding peasants did greatly increase. In southern Italy and coastal Sicily, the relatively wide distribution of property coupled with a cash economy to keep alive poor peasants' dream of becoming small landholders. Those who had never owned land could do so by accumulating some money abroad, and those who had lost their property could hope to regain it by the same method.[28] This dream largely determined patterns of Italian emigration and return migration: Large-scale transoceanic emigration generally took place in Calabria, Abruzzi, Basilicata, and Sicily, all regions where small pieces of land became available for sale. By contrast, northern and central Italy, where large estates were the dominant landholding pattern, saw fewer people leave.[29] From table 3.2 we can discern the relationship between landholding patterns and transoceanic emigration.

Although few central and northern Italians emigrated to the United States, fewer of them returned than their southern compatriots because there were fewer parcels of land to buy in northern Italy. Hence the way for northern Italians to improve their economic lot was to sink roots in the United States.[30] The motivation behind southern Italian emigration—to become small landholders at home—determined that the *contadini* initially did not want to uproot themselves from their native villages but rather eventually to return to those places.[31] Consequently, the majority of these early Italian immigrants coming to the United States were single men.[32] As early as 1884, the *New York Tribune* reporters already discovered the difference between northern and southern Italian immigrants. Northerners, whom the newspaper referred to as "the better class" of Italians, disposed of their property and settled in New York City permanently.[33] Sixteen years later the *Tribune* again noticed this difference:

> Preparations for the return can be seen in the various Italian settlements about the city, but are more noticeable in the Mulberry Bend and Little Italy districts, where most of the Italian laborers live. Over in Bleecker Street, where the Italians from the north of Italy have settled, there is not such a homeward bound movement.[34]

Similarly, the chief goal set by Cantonese peasants in migrating to the

United States was to purchase land in their native villages to enhance their status there. This concern of the New York Chinese was voiced through a 1928 editorial of *Wei Xin Bao (China Reform News)*, a Chinese newspaper published in that city:

> The reason why a Chinese immigrant leaves his motherland and travels thousands of miles abroad is that livelihood back in China is difficult. To leave the native village and to part from one's parents, wife and children, and relatives and friends is a difficult decision to make. Therefore, their purpose in coming to a foreign country is to make a livelihood and money. . . . When an emigrant leaves home, his parents, wife and children, and relatives and friends expect him to be industrious and frugal while abroad, to accumulate money, to keep fit, and to return home as soon as possible to be reunited with his family.[35]

How was the Chinese immigrant going to spend the money that he had accumulated in the United States? A 1946 *Min Qi Ri Bao* editorial, entitled "Where Chinese Immigrants' Savings Will Go," provided a clear answer to this question. "Why should we Chinese immigrants and our families endure all kinds of hardships? Why should we work so hard as to forget all kinds of enjoyment in life?" asked the editorial. "The answer is very simple. Chinese immigrants want

Table 3.2. Landholding Patterns in Italy and Transoceanic Emigration

Regions	Rural Property Concentration Index (1921)	Average Income	Transatlantic Emigration
Emilia-Romagna (Central Italy)	10.8	27	39
Tuscany (Central Italy)	9.0	28	52
Umbria (Central Italy)	6.8	25	52
Marches (Central Italy)	7.9	20	164
Apulia	5.0	18	118
Basilicata (South Italy)	3.2	18	340
Calabria (South Italy)	2.7	16	368
Abruzzi (South Italy)	1.4	17	338
Sicily	3.7	18	263

Source: Josef Barton, *Peasants and Strangers: Italians, Rumanians, and Slovaks in an American City, 1890-1950* (Cambridge, Mass.: Harvard University Press, 1975), 31; J. S. MacDonald, "Agricultural Organization, Migration, and Labor Militancy in Rural Italy," *The Economic History Review*, 2nd. Series, No. 16 (1963), 62; Humbert S. Nelli, *From Immigrants to Ethnics: The Italian Americans* (New York: Oxford University Press, 1982), 32-33.

Table 3.3. Chinese Population in the United States by Sex, 1860-1910

Year	Total	Number		Percent	
		Male	Female	Male	Female
1860	34,933	33,149	1,784	95	5
1870	63,199	58,633	4,566	93	7
1880	105,465	100,686	4,779	95	5
1890	107,488	103,620	3,868	96	4
1900	89,863	85,341	4,522	95	5
1910	71,531	66,856	4,675	93	7

Sources: United States Government, U.S. Bureau of the Census, *Historical Statistics of the United States, Colonial Times to 1970* (White Plains, N.Y.: Kraus International Publishers, 1989), 14.

to accumulate their hard-earned money, penny by penny, and send these savings home to buy land and houses."[36] Ong Yung, a laundry owner in New York, journeyed to China three times during the 1870s to make investments there. By 1885, he was reported to own property worth $15,000 at home.[37] In fact, toward the end of the nineteenth century, quite a few New York Chinese, laundrymen as well as merchants, had purchased land in their native villages. According to a *New York Tribune* report in 1900, during the Boxer Rebellion of that year, many Chinese in New York were anxious to rush home to look after their property, which they feared the anti-foreign Empress Dowager might confiscate.[38] The desire of the New York Chinese to purchase land in their home villages continued during the first half of the twentieth century. In Louis Chu's historical novel on the New York Chinese of the 1940s and early 1950s, *Eat a Bowl of Tea*, we find that all the main figures in the novel cherish a hope to buy land at home.[39]

Since the peasants' final goal was to improve their life in their native villages, Chinese emigration to the United States did not rest on a permanent departure from home. For the great majority of Cantonese immigrants, their journey to the United States was a round-trip. Like Italian emigrants, most Cantonese who came to the United States were single men. In the 1850s, British consulates in the southeastern cities of China were asked to report the status of Chinese emigrants to the government. All the reports pointed to the fact that Chinese emigrants rarely brought families with them. The British consul in Canton reported, "Chinese women never go abroad. . . . The Chinese have a strong attachment to their motherland, which motivates them to be thrifty and to accumulate money for the final return home."[40] Table 3.3 indicates the lack of women among Chinese immigrants.

It should be noted that the lack of women after the mid-1870s was especially due to the discriminatory legislation, like the Page Law and the Chinese Exclusion Act, that barred most Chinese females from entering the

United States.[41] Because of the lack of women in both communities, Little Italys and Chinatown shared certain similar life patterns in their early years. For example, many Italians and a considerable number of Chinese lived in boarding houses.[42] Crowded, filthy apartments as well as vices such as prostitution were common in those days. This similarity between the two communities, however, did not last long. After the turn of the century, more and more Italian immigrants sent for their families, and boarding houses became fewer. But conditions in the Chinese community remained largely unchanged until after World War II when wives of Chinese immigrants were allowed for the first time to join their husbands in the United States.

Did the kind of relationship that Italian emigration shows exist in the landholding patterns in Guangdong and Cantonese emigration to the United States? Several factors prevent our making the confident conclusion that is possible for Italian emigration. One factor is the lack of statistical data on the property ownership index in Si Yi, San Yi, Zhongshan, and other districts in Guangdong. Available sources allow the suggestion that landholding patterns alone do not explain why Chinese emigrants were mostly from San Yi, Si Yi, and Zhongshan. In the early and mid-1920s, the farmers' unions in Guangdong investigated the landholding situation in the province. The result of their investigation is shown in table 3.4.

These reports, however, only covered two of the eight major emigrant counties—Shunde and Panyu. Fortunately, in the late 1920s and early 1930s, Han-sheng Chen, a leading Chinese economist, also investigated landholding in Guangdong. His study provided, among other things, a rural property index for twelve villages in Taishan, a village in Kaiping, six villages in Zhongshan, five in Shunde, and sixty-seven in Panyu. Although Chen only investigated sample villages in each county, the result of his research fairly closely resembles that of the farmers' unions. For example, the percentages of land owners in Shunde, Panyu, and Heshan, as indicated by Chen's reports, were 9 percent, 9 percent, and 6 percent respectively, while the corresponding figures provided by the farmers' unions were 10 percent, 10 percent, and 5 percent. In view of the similarities between the two studies, Chen's data, shown in table 3.5, supplement those given by the farmers' unions.

When tables 3.5 and 3.6 are compared, it becomes clear that areas where land was widely distributed—such as Yangjiang, Wuchuan, Lechang, and Jiaying—were not necessarily emigrant counties. In chapter 2 we pointed out that the location of Si Yi and San Yi—their close proximity to Guangzhou and Hong Kong—was an important reason why Chinese immigrants to the United States mostly originated from this area, rather than from the rest of Guangdong. We still face the question of why San Yi and Si Yi sent uneven numbers of emigrants to the United States. Here, landholding patterns seem to become important. If we focus on the eight sending counties, we find that the emigration patterns are related to the landholding situations there. The San Yi counties—

Table 3.4. Landholding Situation in 12 Districts of Guangdong Province in the Mid-1920s

District	Number of Farmers	Number of Owners	Percentage of Owners
Fengshun	40,136	8,144	20
Chaoyang	56,496	17,455	31
Chaoan	39,053	25,145	64
Chenghai	37,101	16,850	45
Jieyang	38,210	2,153	6
Raoping	86,735	10,885	13
Dabu	16,691	5,281	32
Jiaying	21,977	20,156	92
Changle	14,928	7,240	48
Xingning	137,116	54,313	40
Pingyuan	20,079	4,787	23
Changping	24,066	11,124	47
Xinan	figures not provided		5
Dongguan	figures not provided		5
Heshan	figures not provided		5
Shunde*	figures not provided		10
Panyu*	figures not provided		10

Source: "Kwangtung [Guangdong] Agricultural Statistics," *Chinese Economic Journal*, Published by the Bureau of Industrial and Commercial Information, Ministry of Industry, Commerce, and Labor, National Government of the Republic of China, Vol. II (January to June 1928), 329.

Note: * Indicates counties that sent emigrants to the United States.

Panyu, Shunde, and Nanhai—immediately surround the capital city of Guang-zhou. As one of the richest districts in Guangdong, San Yi was known for a diversified economy consequent on its good topography and its close proximity to the provincial capital. In addition to arable farming, the San Yi residents practiced sericulture and pisciculture, and manufactured silk textiles, ceramics, and handicrafts as well as pursuing commerce.[43] In Shunde, for example, 70 percent of the arable land was devoted to mulberry trees. In the 1920s, the population of this county was 1,800,000, of which at least 1,440,000 (80 percent) were sericulturists.[44] In Nanhai, around 200,000 people out of a total population of 420,000 (47.6 percent) were sericulturists.[45] Such cultivation probably favored the concentration of land in the hands of a small number of people.

By contrast, Si Yi is hilly and its soil barren, which perhaps made large-scale landholding difficult.[46] The economy of Si Yi was much less diversified than San Yi's. Almost all the Si Yi residents were agriculturalists. In Xinhui, for example, only about one tenth of the arable land grew mulberry trees and only 5

Table 3.5. Landholding Situation in Guangdong, 1928-1933

District	No. of Villages	No. of Families	No. of Landowners	% of Owners
Taishan*	12	1,224	224	18
Kaiping*	1	224	112	50
Zhongshan*	6	1,875	435	23
Panyu*	67	26,971	2,536	9
Shunde*	5	3,150	295	9
Yingde	8	474	142	30
Huiyang	2	185	88	48
Meixian	2	275	183	66
Jiaoling	2	265	102	38
Maoming	43	3,191	884	27
Yangjiang	2	129	70	54
Luoding	3	2,900	1,070	37
Wuchuan	2	137	73	53
Huaxien	7	859	113	13
Qujiang	3	798	161	20
Lechang	4	427	249	58

Source: Han-sheng Chen, *Landlord and Peasant in China: A Study of the Agrarian Crisis in South China* (New York: International Publishers, 1936), 115, 116, 117-21.
Note: * Indicates counties that sent most emigrants to the United States.

percent of its population engaged in sericulture.[47] Keeping in mind the proportion of landowners in those areas, it is clear why Si Yi and Zhongshan sent more emigrants to the United States than the San Yi villages—because in Si Yi and Zhongshan the landholding index was higher than that in San Yi. This can be seen in table 3.6.

A high percentage of owners in a population usually meant that land in such an area changed hands more frequently than elsewhere. Taishan, which sent the bulk of the emigrants to the United States, was reported in the late nineteenth century to have experienced many intense struggles over even the hardly arable lands.[48] According to Chen's study, a great part of the remittances sent home from the United States by the Si Yi emigrants was invested in land.[49] Like their Italian counterparts, Chinese immigrants often sent money home before their return. In 1930 alone, the district of Taishan received about 40 million Yuan (approximately U.S. $22 million)[50] from abroad, most of it from the Americas.[51] As a result of the increased investment, land values in Si Yi went up quickly, which in turn led to increases in rents. According to the *Annual of the Taishan District Government* published in 1933, the rent in that county had jumped from 20 Yuan per *mu* in 1928 to 30 Yuan per *mu* in 1933, a 50 percent increase over five years, or 8.5 percent annually.[52] At the same time, Shunde and its neighboring silk districts experienced rent reductions.[53] Conceivably the rent

Table 3.6. Landholding Patterns in Guangdong and Trans-Pacific Migration, 1928-1933

District	No. of Villages	No. of Families	Land owners	% of Owners	Emigration Rates
Taishan (Si Yi)	12	1,224	224	18%	High
Kaiping (Si Yi)	1	224	112	50%	High
Zhongshan	6	1,875	435	23%	High
Panyu (San Yi)	67	26,971	2,536	9%	Low
Shunde (San Yi)	5	3,150	295	9%	Low

Source: Han-sheng Chen, *Landlord and Peasants in China*, 115, 116, 117-21.

reduction in parts of San Yi was a result of falling investment in land.

Money earned in America enabled returned emigrants and their families in Si Yi to hire more farm hands and domestic labor; as a result, both men's and women's wages in Si Yi became substantially higher than those in the rest of the province.[54] As table 3.7 illustrates, the two Si Yi counties, Taishan and Xinhui, clearly stood out by their higher wages for both male and female farm workers. These figures suggest that the Si Yi area witnessed a greater increase in the number of landowners than San Yi. This accords with the much larger group of emigrants sent to the United States by the former. It was also possible that many of the San Yi immigrants were artisans, the people who tended to settle in the United States and therefore did not invest much in land in their native counties.

III

Although the majority of both Italian and Chinese immigrants in New York initially intended to return home, the prevalence of decisions to settle permanently in the United States came much earlier to the Italians than to the Chinese. After the mid-1920s, Italian immigration to New York became a permanent feature, while the sojourner mentality of most of the Chinese continued. The majority of the New York Chinese began to abandon their sojourner mentality only in the early 1950s. This means that they were two and a half decades later than the Italians in making the decision to stay permanently in America. What, then, was the reason for this huge difference in timing? A study of the Italians in San Francisco informs us that these immigrants abandoned their sojourner mentality when their economic opportunity in California became better than that at home.[55] This important clue naturally prompts us to

Table 3.7. Average Wage of Agricultural Day Laborers in Guangdong in Ordinary Seasons, 1936

District	Wages (Yuan)	
	Men	Women
East River		
Huiyang	0.30	0.20
Meixian	0.59	0.37
Jiaoling	0.37	0.25
West River		
Gaoyao	0.60	0.40
Taishan*	0.80	0.56
Xinhui*	0.95	0.65
Panyu*	0.45	0.26
North River		
Yingde	0.29	0.20
Wongyuan	0.30	0.15
Lechang	0.36	0.23
South Western		
Luoding	0.26	0.12
Xinyi	0.17	0.06
Kinxian	0.35	0.25
Fangcheng	0.20	0.10

Source: Chen, *Landlord and Peasant in China*, 105.
Note: * Indicates counties that sent emigrants to the United States.

consider if economic opportunity in New York had anything to do with the abandonment of a goal of return migration among the two immigrant groups there.

In the late nineteenth and early twentieth centuries, manufacturing and construction were the two leading employment opportunities offered in New York. The bulk of Italian immigrants, being unskilled laborers, quickly entered these occupations once in the city.[56] Although few Italian immigrants entered skilled occupations, the number of Italians in certain skilled trades was relatively large.[57] At this time, New York City's economy was growing at an unprecedented rate with new employment opportunities constantly created at every level. As table 3.8 indicates, during the twenty-five years between 1880 and 1905, increasing numbers of Italians seized the new opportunities.

The increase in the skilled and semiskilled categories (18 percent), as Kessner has demonstrated, did not have much to do with the length of residence in the city. Rather, they mostly reflected the fact that many newly arrived Italians had a chance to be trained for skilled occupations and to choose between skilled and unskilled jobs offered in New York.[58] For second generation Italians,

Table 3.8. Occupational Distribution for Italian Household Heads by Number and Percent, New York City, 1880 and 1905

Class		1880		1905		Difference
		Number	Percent	Number	Percent	
I	High White Collar	9	2	23	2.3	+0.3
II	Low White Collar	112	24.9	181	17.8	-7.1
III	Skilled	59	13.1	221	21.8	+8.7
IV	Semiskilled	31	6.9	165	16.3	+9.4
V	Unskilled	239	53.1	425	41.9	-11.2

Source: Thomas Kessner, *The Golden Door: Italian and Jewish Immigrant Mobility in New York City, 1880-1915* (New York: Oxford University Press, 1977), 52, 79, 108-09. Note: Kessner used sample data from Federal Census Schedule for New York and Kings Counties for 1880 and from New York State Census Schedules for New York and Kings Counties, 1905.

Table 3.9. Occupational Distribution for Italian Offspring by Percent, New York City, 1880 and 1905

		1880	1905
I	High White Collar	0.0	0.9
II	Low White Collar	15.4	11.8
III	Skilled	18.6	36.2
IV	Semiskilled	17.6	27.3
V	Unskilled	48.4	23.9
	Total	188.0	586.0
	Total Household Sample	456.0	1,029.0

Source: Thomas Kessner, *The Golden Door*, 79.

who felt less pressure to find immediate employment than their fathers had, the opportunities for moving into the skilled occupations looked more attractive. As table 3.9 indicates, Italian offspring took fuller advantage of New York's opportunities than their parents had.

The trend of upward mobility among Italians continued during the 1910s and 1920s. According to a contemporary study, 50.4 percent of Italian fathers of children born in 1916 were laborers while 22.7 percent of them were engaged in skilled occupations. Fifteen years later, in 1931, the percentage of Italian fathers listed as laborers had dropped to 31.4; in the meantime, those engaged in skilled jobs had increased to 28.3 percent. In 1916, 32.5 percent of Italian bridegrooms in New York were laborers and 28.6 percent of them were skilled workers. By 1931, the corresponding figures had become 10.6 percent for laborers and 32.1 percent for skilled workers. The death records seemed to indicate a similar trend: 22.3 percent of the Italian males deceased in 1916 were laborers; those in the skilled occupation were 17.3 percent. In 1931, 22.2 percent of Italian men deceased were laborers while the percentage of those engaged in the skilled occupations had increased to 20.4 percent.[59]

We should also remember that Italy was devastated by World War I. As shrewd people, Italian immigrants quickly figured out that New York offered an opportunity even better than purchasing land at home. This perhaps explains why, after the turn of the century, increasing number of Italians in this city began to send for their families.[60] On his way from Naples to New York in 1917, a student of Italian emigration discovered that "Italy no good" had become a common saying among virtually all the Italian passengers. "Among the half thousand Italians on board," he observed, "constant inquiry failed to disclose one who had any intention of returning to Italy to live."[61] "I'll never go back to that accursed place," said one of the immigrants, "I can live in New York almost as cheaply as in Naples and make three times as much money."[62] Grace Calabrese, who worked in New York City's garment industry for most of her life, also agreed that to stay in the United States meant a better chance than returning to Italy. "I'm happy what I did," she said. "We struggled. We struggled. We worked very hard, and, you know, today I'm happy with what I did. I don't want to go back and be better than what I was."[63]

In contrast to the Italians, the New York Chinese had few economic opportunities. Most worked in small businesses such as laundries, restaurants, and grocery stores. An 1885 *New York Tribune* report tells us that among the New York Chinese there were 4,500 laundrymen, 300 cigarmakers, 200 sailors, 300 unemployed waiting for an opportunity to open laundries, 100 merchants, and about two dozen other kinds of skilled workers.[64] In 1886, upon visiting New York, the Chinese minister to the United States discovered that most of the Chinese there engaged in the laundry industry.[65] According to the 1930 census, 61 percent of the gainfully employed Chinese in New York State engaged in restaurant or laundry businesses.[66] Since the majority of the New York State Chinese then resided in New York City, the percentage for the city must be fairly close to that for the state. Even by 1946, 60 percent of the New York Chinese still made their living by laundering.[67] The situation remained unchanged by the late 1950s.[68] As a researcher explained later, "For the Chinese in particular, service work today is almost synonymous with such restaurant jobs as cook, waiter, bartender, dishwasher, and the like."[69]

But the majority of Chinese immigrants did not initially arrive in the United States as waiters or laundrymen. Thus the early Chinese immigrants in California engaged in many occupations, including mining, railroad construction, building, clothing, shoemaking, and cigar making. The efforts of organized labor to boycott consumer goods manufactured by Chinese and to force employers to dismiss Chinese workers made the Chinese gradually withdraw from what white workers regarded as their own domain. Chinese immigrants eventually entered occupations that generally did not interest white workers. The contrast between the situations in 1870 and 1920 shown in table 3.10 illustrates

Table 3.10. Change of Chinese Occupations in the United States, 1870-1920

Occupation	Number of Chinese engaged in		Percentage increase or decrease
	1870	1920	
Miners & Laborers	27,045	151	-99.45
Domestic Service	9,349	26,440	+280.00
Traders & Dealers	779	7,477	+960.00

Source: David Te-chao Cheng, *Acculturation of the Chinese in the United States: A Philadelphia Study* (Ph. D. dissertation, University of Pennsylvania, 1948), 59.

drastic change. New York claimed more racial tolerance than California, but for the Chinese there economic opportunities were even a little worse. Wong Chin Foo, a New York Chinese, had found the difference between New York and California as early as 1888:

> In the western states, where their [the Chinese's] value is better under-stood, they are used in as many different positions as any other foreigners, and the laundry business is occupied only by those who fail to find other employment. But here in New York as yet there is no other alternative. Many an able-minded man as well as skilful mechanic who came to America to better his conditions may be found wielding the polishing-irons in a New York Chinese laundry.[70]

Tammany Hall organized anti-coolie rallies in 1870. The *New York Daily Tribune* expressed the following opinion in 1876: "The English, German, Irish, French, and other European immigrants become good citizens and contribute materially to the growth and prosperity of the country. The Chinaman hoards his money in order that he may send it to his native land, and is an unprofitable visitor at best."[71]

It seems that white workers were even reluctant to tolerate the presence of Chinese immigrants in the laundry industry. In March 1890, the Master Laundrymen's Association of New York City held a special meeting that "decided upon a definite plan of campaign against the Chinese." The subcom-mittee "resolved to set in motion a systematic crusade, which should result in removing every laundry operated by Mongolians in New York, Brooklyn, and New Jersey."[72] A resolution was passed that enumerated "the harmful effects of the Chinese in this city." The participants especially resented the fact "that $4,000,000 is annually sent by them [Chinese laundrymen] to China, for which they make no adequate return to this country, and that it is impossible for small laundries to exist in competition with the Chinese cheap laboring men."[73] The resolution that emerged from the meeting was,

> That the presence of the Chinese in this country is an unquestionable local

and national evil, and greatly to the detriment of the white population, morally and socially, and that for the self-protection and preservation of this country and its people, it is the duty of every man and woman, and especially of the great body of working men, mechanics, and business people in general, not to give any work or trade whatsoever to this heathen race.[74]

In 1922, the hostility of white laundrymen toward their Chinese counterparts led to an anti-Chinese campaign in New York City. The immediate cause of this campaign, according to *Wei Xin Bao*, was that the Chinese laundries in Brooklyn were reducing their rates for laundering. Not until the Consolidated Chinese Benevolent Association stepped in and persuaded these laundries to stop reducing prices did the anger of white laundrymen begin to lessen.[75] Another campaign of this kind took place in the early 1930s. As a result of the Great Depression and the introduction of washing machines into laundries, the wages of white laundry workers and the income of laundry owners plummeted. When the Chinese charged less than white laundries' owners and offered additional conveniences such as pick-up and delivery, the outraged white laundrymen responded by posting anti-Chinese cartoons in many places around the city. One of these cartoons portrayed a Chinese laundryman who earned a lot but spent little, and a white laundryman who had to support his family with expensive food. Another pictured a filthy Chinese laundryman at work spitting on a white shirt.[76] Still others displayed the Chinese sending all their earnings back to China.[77] This campaign created many difficulties for the Chinese in New York but it did discourage direct competition.

Under normal circumstances, possessing special skills would promise an immigrant worker a better opportunity for upward mobility because it represented a shortcut leading to the white-collar occupation. This channel, too, was blocked to the Chinese. Before 1940, New York State banned aliens from engaging in almost thirty specific occupations. Though their name was not mentioned, Chinese immigrants must have borne the brunt of this discriminatory legislation because they were not eligible for citizenship. Very often, even second generation Chinese in New York with advanced degrees such as engineering and accounting could not find jobs in U.S. companies but ended up working in Chinese laundries, restaurants, and grocery stores.[78]

With the road to social mobility in the United States blocked, not to mention the harassment from the larger society, the prospect of becoming small landholders in their native villages always looked more attractive to Chinese immigrants than staying in New York.[79] No wonder their wish to return home remained stronger than that of the Italians! As *Xin Bao (China Tribune)*, a New York Chinese newspaper, editorialized in 1946:

The purpose in our coming [to the U.S.] and leaving family members behind in the native villages is to improve our economic life. But the immigration procedure is becoming increasingly difficult and, after entering the U.S., we have to endure racial discrimination. It is not easy to develop our careers here. [Staying in] such an environment is not a solution to our economic problems. If we can build up [a prosperous] Guangdong, then we will be glad to return home to do business there.[80]

Why then did Chinese immigrants collectively begin to change their minds and decide to settle in New York in the early 1950s? Until now historians have not seriously addressed this important question. To answer the question we need to study a series of dramatic changes in the 1940s and early 1950s, especially the changing economic opportunities available to the New York Chinese.

One important factor was World War II, which helped bring some positive changes for the Chinese American community. After the bombing of Pearl Harbor by Japan, China and the United States became allies. China, which had been fighting Japanese aggression for four full years, won admiration from the American public. Meanwhile, the U.S. leaders realized that if China fell it would seriously affect America's war effort in the Pacific. To boost the morale of Chinese troops in their war of resistance, efforts were soon under way to repeal the Chinese Exclusion Act. Congress finally ameliorated this historical mistake in 1943 by giving China an annual immigration quota of 105. Though the quota was too small and in many ways still discriminatory, its significance cannot be neglected: For the first time since 1882, Chinese immigrants could bring families with them to the United States and could be naturalized as U.S. citizens. In addition, the War Brides Act of 1945 enabled many New York Chinese who had served in the U.S. military to bring their fiancées to the United States on a non-quota basis.[81] One of these ex-servicemen was Wang Ben Loy, a protagonist in Louis Chu's *Eat a Bowl of Tea*. Ben Loy served in the military for three years before he was discharged in 1947. He went back to Xinhui to marry Lee Moi Oi in 1948 and brought his bride to New York late that year.[82]

In the meantime, World War II created a labor shortage at home since thousands of white men were sent to the front. Added to this situation was Executive Order 8802, issued by President Franklin Roosevelt in 1941, which outlawed racial discrimination in the defense industry. Consequently, some New York Chinese could find employment in factories and skilled occupations. A major construction company, for example, advertised jobs in a New York Chinese newspaper. By 1942, some Chinese restaurants in New York had to close since many waiters went to work in factories that offered better wages.[83] Although we still lack specific data for New York City, table 3.11 clearly indicates that starting in the early 1940s, the occupational situation of Chinese males in the northeastern United States began to improve.

We should note that the sharp increase in professional and technical occupations probably had less to do with the peasant immigrants than with the

Table 3.11. Changes in Occupations of Chinese American Males, Northeastern United States, 1940-1960

Occupations	Differences by Percentage	
	Foreign-born	Native-born
1. Professional, technical, and kindred workers	+1,200	+625
2. Managers, officials, and proprietors	0	-50
3. Clerical, Sales, and kindred workers	+50	+100
4. Craftsmen, foremen, and kindred workers	+425	+225
5. Operatives and kindred workers	-80	-100
6. Service and domestic workers, laborers	0	-150

Source: D.Y. Yuan, "Regional Changes in Occupational Structure of the Chinese Male Labor Force in the United States, 1940-60," in D. Y. Yuan, *Chinese American Population* (Hong Kong: University of East Asia Press, 1989), 38-39.

large number of Chinese students stranded in New York after the Communist revolution in China in 1949. To a certain extent, this was true of the categories of craftsmen and foremen as well as clerical and sales workers. But categories 2, 5, and 6 in table 3.11 unmistakably indicate some positive changes for the peasant immigrants, because in the New York Chinese community managers and proprietors often meant laundry owners, and operatives and service workers were synonymous with restaurant or laundry employees.

In spite of these positive changes for the New York Chinese community since 1941, the improvements came slowly. When the war was over, for example, many New York Chinese could no longer find factory jobs but returned to their laundry and restaurant businesses.[84] At the same time, housing and other forms of discrimination remained severe. That the improvements were too slow to reverse Chinese immigrants' "sojourner mentality" seems evident from the resumption of return migration when the war with Japan ended in 1945. According to a survey made by the Consolidated Chinese Benevolent Association (CCBA) of San Francisco in 1947, each month about seven hundred Chinese embarked for China through the port there, and a quarter of them would not come back to the United States. The secretary of the CCBA even predicted a fast decline of the Chinese immigrant population in America.[85] The situation of Chinese in the United States further deteriorated during the Korean War in the early 1950s when the immigrants were placed under strict surveillance.[86] If racial hostility had been the only factor affecting Chinese immigrants' lives, they should have continued to return home in the early 1950s. Why did they suddenly decide to stay in America at a time when life was so difficult there? The abandonment of their sojourner mentality, in fact, did not mainly follow from an improvement of the situation in New York but from the closing of economic opportunities at home.

As soon as the Chinese Communists took over Guangdong from the Kuomintang in 1950, they carried out an unprecedented land reform in that province. The land reform itself might be justified by the fact that Chinese peasants had dreamed of becoming small landowners for more than two thousand years. The key question, however, was how to deal with Guangdong's special situation vis-à-vis that of the rest of China. The early policy makers for the land reform in Guangdong did notice that overseas Chinese and their families made up 20 percent of that province's population, and that much land in Guangdong was possessed by overseas Chinese.[87] These moderates made a careful distinction between people who had been landlords before migrating abroad and those who became landowners after returning from overseas with the money earned in foreign countries. Had this moderate line prevailed, then due allowance would probably have been given to the people in the second category who had worked for the money to buy their land. But, for reasons beyond the scope of this book, a leftist line came to dominate the policy making and land reform in Guangdong suddenly took a radical turn.

To the Chinese immigrants in New York, the message from the land reform in Guangdong was unequivocal: Because many of them had purchased land at home, they became the targets of the land reform. This means that, as landlords, their land was soon to be confiscated. For almost a whole year in 1951, the reports carried by *Min Qi Ri Bao* on the land reform in Si Yi riveted the attention of all Chinese immigrants in New York. What also scared the immigrants was the political denunciation directed towards the landowners, which in Guangdong included returned immigrants. According to one report, 40 percent of the 990,000 people of Taishan were denounced and 20 percent related to landlords were put under strict surveillance.[88]

It should be observed that, considering *Min Qi Ri Bao*'s pro-Kuomintang stance, exaggerations of the atrocities were indeed not impossible and, in fact, the pro-Communist *Mei Zhou Hua Qiao Ri Bao* lost no time in coming out to defend the radical land reform.[89] *Mei Zhou Hua Qiao Ri Bao* also explained to its readers why the division of land could not be carried out peacefully. "To divide the land peacefully," reasoned the newspaper, "is like asking a tiger for its skin. . . . The landlords will never willingly renounce their land."[90] Nevertheless, *Mei Zhou Hua Qiao Ri Bao* did not deny the fact that Cantonese immigrants' land was being confiscated. As a matter of fact, this newspaper went even so far as to declare that "there is no reason to maintain Chinese immigrant landlords' feudal and exploitative landowning system."[91]

The open and generous admission in recent years by leaders of the Communist Party of excesses in Guangdong's land reform by their predecessors some forty years before should settle controversy over the excesses of that earlier policy.[92] They admit, for example, that 70 percent of the family members of overseas Chinese in Guangdong were wrongly punished during the land reform.[93] In Kaiping County alone, according to the county's party secretary, 2,179 people were wrongly punished and 299 people were executed by mistake.[94]

By the end of 1951, the Chinese in New York as well as in the rest of the United States were faced with two choices. On the one hand, if they returned home they would face the reality that the land they had purchased had been confiscated. On the other hand, economic opportunities in New York had improved slightly from ten years before. Not surprisingly, almost all of them chose to stay. Chu's *Eat A Bowl of Tea* offers perhaps the best description of how the New York Chinese reluctantly remained in New York in the early 1950s. The experience of Lee Gong, one of the main figures in the novel, was typical:

> Some ten years later [1938], he sold his laundry. With the proceeds from the sale of the laundry plus his small savings, he had planned to spend the late evening of his life in the rural quiet of Sunwei [Xinhui]. The Sino-Japanese war had prevented him from realizing this long-cherished goal. The unsettled conditions of subsequent years in the far east, which saw Mao Tse-tung grab control of the Central Government of China from Chiang Kai-shek, had weighed heavily in his decision not to return to Sunwei [Xinhui]. While there were intermittent periods of peaceful travel in China for those who wanted it, Lee Gong could not bring himself to see anything permanently stable for a retired Gimshunhock [a guest from the gold mountains] in China. So reluctantly he remained in New York.[95]

IV

In sum, with admittedly scant sources, we seem a step closer toward substantiating the hypothesis on the parallels of European and Chinese emigration. In many ways Chinese immigration to New York did parallel its Italian counterpart: In both cases, the areas where land was fairly widely distributed (and thus potentially available for purchase) sent most emigrants to the United States; in both cases, the artisans and skilled workers preceded the peasants in migrating to America; and in both cases, the artisans and skilled workers tended to settle in the United States while the majority of the peasant immigrants were inclined to return home.

In terms of abandoning their sojourner mentality, the two immigrant groups also shared some similarity. Both the Italians and the Chinese carefully weighed the choices at their disposal and, upon discovering that economic opportunities in New York had become better than those at home, they both made the decision to remain in the United States. The fact that despite continued injustices against them in the early 1950s the Chinese still chose to stay in New York indefinitely indicates that surviving legal discrimination and harassment was not the only concern of Chinese immigrants. In addition to these injustices, the Chinese had to worry about their livelihood, and they constantly made choices between the two kinds of survival. Before the early 1950s, to return to their native villages in Guangdong provided the immigrants escape from discrimination in America and a better life at home. But after the early 1950s, the closing of economic opportunities at home became even less endurable than the various injustices in the United States. Therefore, they chose to stay in America.

Notes

1. See Chan, "European and Asian Immigration into the United States in Comparative Perspective," 38-39.

2. Gunther Barth, for example, has observed that "the sojourners' pursuit of their limited goal influenced the reception of the Chinese in the United States who were, as a result, excluded from the privileges and obligations of other immigrants." See Barth, *Bitter Strength*, 1.

3. Roger Daniels "Westerners from the East: Oriental Immigrants Reappraised," *Pacific Historical Review*, Vol. XXXV, No. 4 (November 1966), 375-76. In another article Daniels also expressed this concern. See Daniels, "American Historians and East Asian Immigrants," in *The Asian American: The Historical Experience*, ed. Norris Hundley, Jr. (Santa Barbara: American Bibliographical Center—Clio Press, 1976), 6, 10-11.

4. Franklin Ng, "The Sojourner, Return Migration, and Immigration History," *Chinese America: History and Perspectives* (San Francisco: Chinese Historical Society of America, 1987), especially 60-63.

5. Chan, "European and Asian Immigration in Comparative Perspective," 38-44.

6. Louis J. Beck, *New York's Chinatown: A Historical Presentation of Its People and Places* (New York: Bohemia Publishing Company, 1898), 193-94.

7. Cheng-tsu Wu, "Chinese People and Chinatown in New York City" (Ph.D. dissertation, Clark University, 1958), 26. Indeed, the tendency among Chinese immigrants to return home was so pervasive that if they happened to die overseas before realizing their dream of returning, their last wish was to have their remains carried back to their native villages. See *New York Times*, 25 June 1888. Also see *Wei Xin Bao*, 26 December 1917 and 13 March 1918; *Guo Quan Bao*, 30 April 1933.

8. The Kuomintang, or the Nationalist Party, was the ruling party in China from 1928 to 1949. KMT is an abbreviation for the Kuomintang.

9. *Min Qi Ri Bao*, 8 and 9 February 1945. It is not altogether clear why, as early as 1945, the pro-KMT immigrants tried to keep Chinese communities in the United States. It might be possible that, foreseeing the likelihood of a civil war in China following the victory over Japan, some pro-KMT elites in Chinatown hoped to keep an overseas base for the party in case the KMT lost the war. However, no matter what these people's motivation was, it is clear that the majority of Chinese immigrants in New York wanted to return to China after the war with Japan. For more contemporary reports on the anxiety of the New York Chinese to return home after the war with Japan, see *Xin Bao*, 13 August 1945, and 22 and 23 May 1946.

10. Before the 1950s, all New York Chinese newspapers dated their publications by the

Chinese Republican calendar. The year 1938, for example, was expressed in the form of the twenty-seventh year of the Chinese Republic because the Republic of China was founded in 1912 and that year was referred to as the first year of the Chinese Republic. Even in the 1990s, some New York Chinese newspapers that did not have a pro-mainland tendency still used the calendar of the Chinese Republic.

11. The five major newspapers, *Guo Quan Bao, Wei Xin Bao, Min Qi Ri Bao, Mei Zhou Hua Qiao Ri Bao,* and *Xin Bao* had special pages and columns exclusively devoted to the news about Guangdong Province and Si Yi, from which most New York Chinese originated. The Chinese in New York and the prefects of their respective hometowns, especially Taishan County, frequently corresponded, discussing the defense, welfare, and construction of those counties. For several examples, see *Guo Quan Bao,* 4 March 1922; *Mei Zhou Hua Qiao Ri Bao,* 14 February 1942, 19 and 21 January 1943, 15 May 1943; and *Min Qi Ri Bao,* 26 October 1943.

12. *Harper's Weekly,* 23 November 1889. For similar comments see *New York Tribune,* 23 November 1884 and *Harper's Weekly,* 18 October 1890.

13. Caroline Ware, *Greenwich Village, 1920-1930: A Comment on American Civilization in the Post-War Years* (Boston: Houghton Mifflin, 1935), 154, 156.

14. Gaspare Cusumano, "Study of the Colony of Cinisi in New York City," in *Old World Traits Transplanted,* ed. Park and Miller, 150.

15. Cusumano, "Study of the Colony of Cinisi in New York City," 150-51.

16. This kind of classification disappeared in the late 1930s, which coincided with and perhaps even symbolized the decreasing significance of provincialism and the sojourner mentality among Italian immigrants.

17. *United America,* 24 October 1925. By 1926, according to *United America,* there were only about 12,000 Italians in the United States whose wives and children still remained in Italy. This is an insignificant figure when we consider that in 1920 there were 1,610,000 foreign-born Italians in the United States. See *United America,* 12 June 1926.

18. *New York Daily Tribune,* 2 June 1895. According to the same report, many Italians were at this time already deciding to stay permanently in the New World. Although exaggerated, this statement does show a difference between Italian and Chinese immigrants, the latter reversing their sojourner mentality much later than the former.

19. Gino C. Speranza, "The Effect of Emigration on Italy: An Interview with Adolfo Rossi," in *The Italians,* ed. Cordasco and Bucchioni, 89.

20. Rudolph M. Bell, *Fate and Honor, Family and Village: Demographic and Cultural Change in Rural Italy since 1880* (Chicago: University of Chicago Press, 1979), 179.

21. Foerster, *The Italian Emigration of Our Times,* 417.

22. Foerster, *The Italian Emigration of Our Times,* 428. See also Dino Cinel, *From Italy to San Francisco: The Immigrant Experience* (Stanford: Stanford University Press, 1982), 35-96.

23. Giuseppe Giacosa, *Impressioni D'America* (Milano: Tipografia Editrice L.F. Cogliati, 1898), 171.

24. Quoted in Cinel, *From Italy to San Francisco,* 60.

25. Gino C. Sperenza, "Political Representation of Italo-American Colonies in the Italian Parliament," *Charities,* Vol. 15 (1906), 521, in *The Italians,* ed. Cordasco and Bucchioni, 309.

60

Chapter 3

26. Cinel, *From Italy to San Francisco*, 61; Josef Barton, *Peasants and Strangers: Italians, Rumanians, and Slovaks in an American City, 1890-1950* (Cambridge, Mass.: Harvard University Press, 1975), 28-29; J.S. MacDonald, "Agricultural Organization, Migration and Labor Militancy in Rural Italy," *The Economic History Review*, 2nd. Series, No. 16 (1963), 65-66.

27. Barton, *Peasants and Strangers*, 28, 30, 35, 36; J.S. MacDonald, "Agricultural Organization, Migration and Labor Militancy in Rural Italy," 72; and Cinel, *From Italy to San Francisco*, 61.

28. Barton, *Peasants and Strangers*, 30.

29. Italian immigrants, in fact, were a group of calculating people. They knew exactly when they would leave and when to return. Contrary to the common assumption that peasants emigrated during hard times, it was when the harvest was good that they left. Only during good times could the *contadini* save enough money for their trips. See Bell, *Fate and Honor, Family and Village*, 186-87.

30. *New York Tribune*, 23 November 1884. See also *New York Tribune*, 9 September 1900.

31. Foerster, *The Italian Emigration of Our Times*, 41.

32. From the 1870s to the 1910s, the proportion of females to the total Italian immigrants was always between 20 and 25 percent. See *Reports of the Immigration Commission*, Vol. 4, *Emigration Conditions in Europe* (Washington, D.C., 1911), 138.

33. *New York Tribune*, 23 November 1884.

34. *New York Tribune*, 9 September 1900.

35. *Wei Xin Bao*, 7 March 1928.

36. *Min Qi Ri Bao*, 9 August 1946.

37. *New York Tribune*, 21 June 1885.

38. *New York Tribune*, 24 July 1900.

39. Louis Chu, *Eat a Bowl of Tea* (Seattle: University of Washington Press, 1961), 24.

40. *Hua Gong Chu Guo Shi Liao Hui Bian (Sources of Chinese Emigration)*, ed. Han-sheng Chen, Vol. 2, (Beijing: Zhong Hua Shu Ju, 1980), 9.

41. The Page Law, passed by Congress in 1875, was initially meant to prohibit the migration of prostitutes into the United States. In reality, however, the law excluded not only Chinese prostitutes but other Chinese women as well. When the Chinese Exclusion Act was ratified in 1882, Chinese women were completely denied entry. See George A. Peffer, "Forbidden Families: Emigration Experiences of Chinese Women under the Page Law, 1875-1882," *Journal of American Ethnic History* (fall 1986), 28-46; Sucheng Chan, "The Exclusion of Chinese Women, 1870-1943," in *Entry Denied: Exclusion and the Chinese Community in America, 1882-1943*, ed. Sucheng Chan, (Philadelphia: Temple University Press, 1991), especially 105-32; Ronald Takaki, *Strangers from a Different Shore*, 40; Judy Yung, *Unbound Feet: A Social History of Chinese Women in San Francisco* (Berkeley: University of California Press, 1995), 23-24.

42. See, for example, *Harper's Weekly*, 1 December 1888, 918.

43. Thomas W. Chinn, *A History of the Chinese in California: A Syllabus* (San Francisco: Chinese Historical Society of America, 1969), 2.

44. "The Silk Industry in Kwangtung [Guangdong] Province," *Annals of the Chinese*

Economy (published by the Chinese Nationalist Government), Vol.V. (1929), 607.

45. "The Silk Industry in Kwangtung [Guangdong] Province," *Annals of the Chinese Economy*, 610. The data for Panyu were incomplete.

46. Chan, *This Bittersweet Soil*, 18.

47. "The Silk Industry in Kwangtung [Guangdong] Province," *Annals of the Chinese Economy*, 612.

48. *Annals of Xin-ning (Taishan)*, compiled in 1893, Taipei reprint edition (Taipei: 1968), Vol. 26, No. 3, 11-12. Cited in Robert G. Lee, "The Origins of Chinese Immigration to the United States, 1848-1882," in *The Life, Influence and the Role of the Chinese in the United States, 1776-1960*, 185.

49. Han-sheng Chen, *Landlord and Peasant in China: A Study of the Agrarian Crisis in South China* (New York: International Publishers, 1936), 67.

50. This exchange rate is calculated on the basis of the data provided by *Economic Facts*, a publication of the Department of Agricultural Economics, University of Nanjing, September 1936 to April 1946, 6.

51. Chen, *Landlord and Peasant in China*, 84.

52. Chen, *Landlord and Peasant in China*, 67.

53. Chen, *Landlord and Peasant in China*, 67. It is not clear whether by "its neighboring silk districts" Chen meant the other two San Yi counties, Nanhai and Panyu—most likely he did.

54. Chen, *Landlord and Peasant in China*, 104.

55. Cinel, *From Italy to San Francisco*, 124.

56. In the 1910s, Italian males in New York predominated in the Street Cleaning Department, subway construction work, and building trades. In 1900, 77 percent of the women workers of Italian parentage engaged in manufacturing. See John H. Mariano, *The Italian Contribution to American Democracy* (Boston: The Christopher Publishing House, 1921), 33, and Louise Odencrantz, *Italian Women in Industry: A Study of Conditions in New York City* (New York: Russell Sage Foundation, 1919), 32-33.

57. See George Pozzetta, "The Italians of New York City, 1890-1914" (Ph.D. dissertation, University of North Carolina at Chapel Hill, 1971), 306-07.

58. Kessner, *The Golden Door*, 108-09.

59. John J. D'Alesandre, "Occupational Trends of Italians in New York City," *Italy-America Monthly*, Vol. 2 (February 25, 1935), 11-21.

60. In fact, some Italian immigrants began to send for their families in the late 1880s. See Bernard J. Lynch, "The Italians in New York," *The Catholic World*, 47, (April, 1888), 67; see also *New York Tribune*, 2 June 1895. Kessner's study of Italian lodgers in New York City reveals that in 1880, 71.4 percent of the boarders were unrelated to the families they were living with. By 1905, not only had the proportion of boarders fallen to half of the 1880 level, but also half of the lodgers were relatives. These changes tell us that by 1905, many Italian host families had sent for their own relatives. At the same time, many boarders had been joined by their family members in New York. See Kessner, *The Golden Door*, 100-02.

61. Willard Price, "What I Learned by Travelling from Naples to New York in the Steerage," in *The Italians*, ed. Cordasco and Bucchioni, 105.

62. Price, "What I learned by Travelling from Naples to New York," in *The Italians*,

ed. Cordasco and Bucchioni, 105.

63. Joan Morrison and Charlotte Fox Zabusky, *American Mosaic: The Immigrant Experience in the Words of Those Who Lived It* (New York: Dutton, 1980), 65.

64. *New York Tribune*, 21 June 1885.

65. Yin-huan Zhang, "San Zhou Ri Ji (Diaries of Travelling the Three Continents)," Vol. 1, in *Hua Gong Chu Guo Shi Liao*, ed. Han-shang Chen, Vol. 4, 578. See also Wong Chin Foo, "The Chinese in the United States," *Chautauguan*, October 1888 to July 1889, 215-17, cited in Renqiu Yu, *To Save China, to Save Ourselves: A History of the Chinese Hand Laundry Alliance of New York City* (Philadelphia: Temple University Press, 1992), 207.

66. United States Government, U.S. Bureau of the Census, *The Fifteenth Census, 1930, Population*, Vol.V, *General Report on Occupations* (Washington, D.C.: Government Printing House, 1931), 95-97.

67. *Mei Zhou Hua Qiao Ri Bao*, 19 December 1946.

68. *Mei Zhou Hua Qiao Ri Bao*, 12 April 1958.

69. Betty Lee Sung, *A Survey of Chinese-American Manpower and Employment* (New York: Praeger, 1976), 81.

70. Wong Chin Foo, "The Chinese in New York," 298.

71. *New York Daily Tribune*, 1 July 1876.

72. *New York Times*, 18 March 1890.

73. *New York Tribune*, 18 March 1890.

74. *New York Times*, 21 March 1890. No report was made, however, on the result of the proposal.

75. *Wei Xin Bao*, 6 September 1922.

76. *Guo Quan Bao*, 20 December 1931.

77. *Guo Quan Bao*, 5 June 1932.

78. For examples of how educated Chinese youth in New York were discriminated against in seeking employment, see Betty Lee Sung, *Mountain of Gold*, 242; see also Julia Chen, "The Chinese Community in New York, 1920-1940" (Ph.D. dissertation, American University, 1941), 100, 158-60.

79. Sung, *Mountain of Gold*, 240.

80. *Xin Bao*, 5 April 1946.

81. Roger Daniels, *Asian America*, 306; Ronald Takaki, *Strangers from a Different Shore*, 378, 417.

82. Chu, *Eat a Bowl of Tea*, 27, 44.

83. See *Xin Bao*, 30 May 1944; see also Takaki, *Strangers from a Different Shore*, 374.

84. Jian-xiong Wu, *Hai Wai Yi Min Yu Hua Ren She Hui (Chinese Emigration and Overseas Chinese Community)* (Taipei: Yun Chen, 1994), 267, footnote 52. Wu had interviewed quite a few Chinese ex-servicemen in New York.

85. *Mei Zhou Hua Qiao Ri Bao*, 24 July 1947.

86. Takaki, *Strangers from a Different Shore*, 415.

87. Jiang-ming Zhang, *Li Shi Zhuan Zhe Guan Tou de Ye Jian Ying (Ye Jian Ying at the Historical Turning Point)* (Beijing: Zhong Gong Dang Shi Chu Ban She, 1997), 90-93, 107, 128, 132.

88. *Min Qi Ri Bao*, 2 November 1951.
89. *Mei Zhou Hua Qiao Ri Bao*, 4 January 1952.
90. *Mei Zhou Hua Qiao Ri Bao*, 23 January 1952.
91. *Mei Zhou Hua Qiao Ri Bao*, 15 September 1952.
92. Zhang, *Li Shi Zhuan Zhe Guan Tou de Ye Jian Ying*, 128-32.
93. Zhang, *Li Shi Zhuan Zhe Guan Tou de Ye Jian Ying*, 129.
94. Zhang, *Li Shi Zhuan Zhe Guan Tou de Ye Jian Ying*, 132.
95. Chu, *Eat a Bowl of Tea*, 17-18.

4

Living Close to Work

Scholars who examine the residential patterns of Chinese living in New York City often assume that most Chinese lived in New York's Chinatown before the mid-1960s.[1] They argue that along with the common culture that attracted the Chinese to live together in Chinatown, both hegemonic housing discrimination and racial hostilities against Chinese corralled these immigrants into a single neighborhood. In his important study of the segregation of New York Chinatown, one scholar has emphasized two fundamental reasons for the concentration of Chinese in the enclave: to develop a kind of defensive insulation against hostilities from the larger society and to preserve the Chinese way of life.[2] Yvonne M. Lau developed her argument along the same line. She has observed in a 1976 article that "it [New York's Chinatown] grew out of both social needs to maintain cultural forms of traditional China, inherent especially to southeastern Chinese society, and out of protective needs to countervail anti-Chinese hostilities."[3] But while such an argument for high concentrations of Chinese in Chinatown holds for the Chinese in other cities such as San Francisco, the New York Chinese actually followed a different residential pattern. During the first half of the twentieth century, more and more of the New York Chinese chose, perhaps reluctantly, to live in neighborhoods dominated by the white majority where discrimination remained rampant. After the mid-1960s, when racial discrimination was diminishing, increasing numbers of the New York Chinese took up residence in Chinatown. This seemingly paradoxical phenomenon prompts us to ask what other possible factors affected Chinese immigrants' residential choices.

This chapter demonstrates that several factors affected Chinese immigrants' residential choices. In addition to any need to avoid housing discrimination and white neighbors' harassment, their workplaces had had a crucial impact on the immigrants' residential location choices since the 1880s when the New York Chinese community began. A simple truth is that the Chinese, like other immigrants, needed to work and wished to live as close to their workplaces as feasible. In New York City the economically marginalized Chinese could work only in laundries and restaurants and these had to be scattered to be close to their customers. Thus, with more and more Chinese firms established outside Chinatown, increasing numbers of New York Chinese took up residence near to them and, by default, in white neighborhoods.

The situation became complex after the early 1960s. On the one hand, some older immigrants moved back to Chinatown where better housing had become available and where they hoped to get good educations for their children. On the other hand, the 1960s witnessed the arrival of thousands of new Chinese immigrants in New York as a result of the 1965 Immigration Act. These newcomers mostly settled in Chinatown because of the language barriers and higher rents in other areas. During this decade, the Chinese garment industry became the leading Chinese American business in the city. The owners of the garment industries located their factories in Chinatown where they could find a supply of laborers who were reluctant to leave the enclave to seek employment in other areas of the city. Consequently, the majority of the new immigrants worked in Chinatown's clothing factories and restaurants, and the proportion of Chinese living in Chinatown actually became higher than that before the 1960s.

I

A common culture had indeed encouraged many early Chinese to choose Chinatown to live. It is generally believed that New York Chinatown started with a Chinese grocery store named Wo Kee, which went into business near Cherry Street in the 1870s. Wo Kee moved a few times and eventually settled in Mott Street. Nearly all the New York Chinese resided around the store then.[4] Lower rents probably lured the Chinese to settle in this ghetto area that Irish and Jewish immigrants had recently vacated. At that time, the small number of New York Chinese included cigarmakers, cigar vendors, grocers, and laundrymen.[5] The small number of Chinese businesses probably did not result in sharp competition, and its absence made it possible for the immigrants to concentrate around Mott Street.

Beginning in the early 1880s, large groups of Chinese migrated from California to New York to avoid the escalating anti-Chinese movements on the West Coast.[6] Consequently, the need for Chinese goods greatly increased. By the late 1880s, New York had more than thirty Chinese grocery stores, all located in, or near, Mott Street.[7] This was probably the period when some Chinese began to disperse to other parts of the city. But these groceries were usually also headquarters of Chinese social organizations and many New York Chinese continued to live around them as they needed a place, like Chinatown, to socialize with their fellow countrymen.[8] Lower rents and a common culture thus contributed to the formation of New York Chinatown. Yet other factors, more powerful than a common culture, pushed the Chinese toward Chinatown.

For many decades, the New York Chinese were victims of housing discrimination. As early as 1869, a *New York Times* reporter had noticed how discrimination in housing forced Chinese immigrants into congested tenements in the Lower East Side:

> They [Chinese immigrants] reside chiefly in Baxter, Mulberry, and Cherry Streets, and are driven much to those filthy localities by the unwillingness of landlords anywhere to receive them on account of their color. Even where they are admitted as tenants they are charged higher rents than whites, and pay $10 a month for a room that an American or European would pay but $6 for.[9]

In 1880, *New York Sun* reported that the Chinese had great difficulty "procuring buildings for habitations and business purposes in any desirable part of town."[10] At the same time, living in white vicinities involved risks such as assault by their neighbors. In 1881, on his way back to his laundry after attending Sunday School on West 23rd Street, Yung Ley Teep was assaulted by a group of gangsters at the intersection of Spring and Marion Streets. His attackers beat him, kicked him, and finally stabbed him. Yung died in hospital two weeks after the assault.[11] In 1900, a crowd of young men and boys attacked a Chinese laundry at 53rd Street and 9th Avenue with sticks, stones, bricks, and tomatoes. According to a *New York Tribune* report, "Windows were broken and the Chinamen were driven into hiding. . . . The police did not appear on the scene and no arrests were made."[12] A year later, the *New York Tribune* observed that "to attack Chinese laundries is a form of amusement very popular in certain quarters [of New York City]."[13]

The hostility of white workers can hardly have been irrelevant to the decision of the Chinese of where to live. Earlier we mentioned the decision of the Master Laundrymen's Association of New York City in 1890 to remove every Chinese laundry in New York, Brooklyn, and New Jersey.[14] Perhaps not sure they would be able to achieve the goal, the association urged the Board of Aldermen to pass an ordinance to restrict the Chinese to certain districts of the city.[15] A few years later, the Women's Rescue League of New York and the Independent Shirt Ironers and Laundry Workers' Union also launched a campaign aimed at Chinese laundrymen.[16] Citywide campaigns targeting Chinese laundries also occurred during the 1920s and 1930s.[17] White workers' hostilities and efforts to limit Chinese laundries to certain districts in the city must have inclined, even driven, these Asian immigrants to live in Chinatown if they could.

Housing discrimination and harassment against Chinese did not begin to diminish until after World War II. "Until the nineteen-forties," recalled a long-time resident of New York Chinatown, "we couldn't buy a house outside [Chinatown]. New York had no law against it, as some states did—it was just discrimination."[18] While working in a laundry on 82nd Street in the 1940s, Sin

Jang Leung was often assaulted by white youth. "White boys picked on Chinese laundrymen," Leung recalled later. Once when he was about to go to Chinatown to celebrate Chinese New Year after a day's work, several white boys hurled a slop can at Leung. Missing him, the can smashed the front window of his laundry.[19]

The residential segregation of the New York Chinese in a way resembled that of African Americans during their migration from the rural South to the urban North in the early twentieth century. The settling of the blacks in Harlem, New York City, highlighted how racial hostility transformed a white neighborhood into a segregated black ghetto. As increasing numbers of blacks took up residence in Harlem, white residents coalesced to resist what they called a black "invasion." Some property owners proposed to evict all blacks from Harlem and forbid further sales or rentals of property to African Americans.[20] Despite such hostilities, more and more blacks moved into Harlem. Whites' response was to evacuate the neighborhood. Between 1920 and 1930, approximately 120,000 white residents left Harlem and about 90,000 African Americans moved in. By 1930, 72 percent of Manhattan's black population lived in Harlem. Once they had settled in Harlem, blacks seldom had a chance to escape the ghetto; poverty and discrimination prevented them from finding better housing elsewhere in the city.[21]

Until 1910, Chicago's white residents had tolerated the presence of small numbers of blacks in their neighborhoods. Later as the black population increased and as its members tried to find adequate housing in the city, white hostility began. Through intimidation, buying property, and plain violence, whites tried to force blacks out of the neighborhoods that they saw as white areas. When these efforts failed, white residents moved out, as their counterparts in Harlem were later to do. By 1915, an almost exclusive black enclave on the South Side of the city plus a small offshoot on the West Side housed most of Chicago's blacks.[22]

Although a common culture, housing discrimination, and white workers' hostility were important reasons for many Chinese to concentrate in Chinatown in the late nineteenth century,[23] the same factors do not explain why, in the following decades, an increasing number of them chose to live outside Chinatown. Table 4.1 portrays the situation.

We should remember that the dispersion of Chinese to white neighborhoods occurred from the 1900s to the 1940s, when housing and other forms of discrimination against them prevailed.[24] In view of the attendant risks, a question naturally arises: What motivated more and more New York Chinese to leave Chinatown and endure discrimination in white neighborhoods? Apparently, factors other than a common culture, housing discrimination, and harassment affected Chinese immigrants' residential location choices. Here a review of Italian immigrants' residential choices proves helpful. As with the

Table 4.1. Proportion of Chinese Living Outside New York's Chinatown, 1920 to 1960

	1920	1930	1940	1950	1960
New York City (total)	5,042	8,414	12,752	18,327	32,831
Outside Chinatown	2,127	4,959	7,588	15,147	18,559
Percentage	42.2	58.9	59.5	82.6	56.5

Source: United States Government, U.S. Bureau of the Census, *The Fourteenth Census, 1920, Population* (Washington, D.C.: Government Printing House, 1922), Vol. III, 679, 714; *The Fifteenth Census, 1930*, Vol. III, 297; Welfare Council of New York City, *Population in Health Areas, New York City* (New York: Research Bureau, Welfare Council of New York City, 1931), 6; *The Sixteenth Census, 1940*, Vol. II, Part V, 157; *Population and Housing Statistics for the Health Area, New York City* (Washington, D.C.: n.p., 1942), 108; *The Seventeenth Census, 1950*, Vol. II, Part XXXII, 171; *The Eighteenth Census, 1960*, Vol. I, 107; *Census Data with Maps for Small Areas of New York City, 1910-1960*, ed. Benjamin P. Bowser, Evelyn S. Mann, and Martin Oling, in microfilm (Ithaca, NY.: n. p., 1981), 86, 114, and Map 1-B.

Chinese, common culture and housing discrimination motivated many New York Italians to cluster in their ethnic neighborhoods. As the following chapter discusses in more detail, Italians preferred to live on the same New York streets as their fellow townsmen. These southern Europeans encountered housing discrimination, although to a lesser degree than that suffered by the New York Chinese. Marie Concistré, an Italian American social worker in New York, was refused an apartment in the early 1940s because the superintendent did not like her Italian surname. To be denied housing in non-Italian neighborhoods, observed Concistré in 1941, was "a common occurrence for the last 40 years among Italians, or American-born children of Italian parentage."[25] Some southern Italian immigrants did manage to rent or purchase houses in non-Italian neighborhoods. But their experience there was not a happy one. As one of them observed after his father purchased a new house in Brooklyn:

> Thus, when my father bought his house he was told exactly the same thing told to my grandfather and also told me in my neighborhood, "we don't want too many of your kind here." In all the time I grew up in this WASP neighborhood I can never recall being invited into anybody's home despite the fact that my father was quite the item. . . . Everyone was very polite, very genteel, but there was always some fear that we might miscegenate.[26]

Undoubtedly, the difficulty of finding housing in non-Italian neighborhoods contributed to these immigrants' concentration in the Little Italys. On top of these factors, the immigrant workers' desire to be close to their workplaces motivated Italians to cluster in the Little Italys, especially the one along Mulberry Street.[27] In the late nineteenth and early twentieth centuries this was especially clear because the public transportation system in New York remained relatively underdeveloped. In the 1890s, 64 percent of the New York Italians lived in the Bowery Street area in lower Manhattan; only 10 percent of them established homes in East Harlem. This disproportion reflects the fact that the area below 14th Street in lower Manhattan held 67 percent of New York City's factory jobs during this period.[28] In 1911, according to a contemporary investigation, 62 percent of male and 76 percent of female Italian workers lived in lower Manhattan below 14th Street. This investigation also informs us that 55 percent of Italian men and 75 percent of Italian women employed in lower Manhattan walked to their workplaces.[29]

Italian experience in Elizabeth Street of lower Manhattan presented a typical example of living close to work: A large number of Italian garment workers, men and women, concentrated in this neighborhood because it was close to a clothing factory between Broome and Spring Streets.[30] Of course, for various reasons, some people did not live close to their workplaces. But even in this case, proximity to workplaces figured in choices of living places. In the Bronx, for example, many Italians lived near the main transportation lines, a clear sign of their desire to get to work easily.[31]

The preference for living close to work was expressed in the residential patterns of other immigrant groups in New York City as well. For many years in the late nineteenth century, Eastern European Jews concentrated in the Lower East Side of Manhattan because most of them worked in the garment industry and most clothing factories were located there.[32] In the 1910s when the garment factories moved to midtown Manhattan, Brooklyn, and the Bronx, the Jews, following jobs and pursuing better housing, left the Lower East Side en masse. By 1925, for example, the Jewish population in Brownsville, Brooklyn, had surpassed 200,000. Most of the Jews here were skilled garment workers employed in the neighborhood's clothing factories.[33] Although for many Jews the movement out of the Lower East Side meant a separation of home and work, newly completed transit lines could facilitate their journey to work and the workers tried to find housing close to the transit line.[34]

The importance of the workplace in affecting residential patterns also explains the movement of many Italians out of lower Manhattan after World War I: The transplantation of factories to other boroughs speeded up immediately after the war. From table 4.2 we can discern the trend of Italian immigrants moving out of the Little Italys in Manhattan and heading for other boroughs from 1920 to 1950.

In studying Chinese immigrants' residential location choices, we should keep in mind the importance of economic survival: Chinese immigrants had to work and, predictably, most of them preferred to live close to their workplaces. Economic influences, especially the location of the workplace, became a decisive determinant of Chinese immigrants' residential patterns.

From the onset of the New York Chinese community, racism limited the Chinese to a few service occupations, especially laundry work. In the late 1880s,

Table 4.2. Number and Proportion of Foreign-Born Italians Living in the Five Boroughs of New York City, 1920-1950

	1920	1930	1940	1950
New York City	390,832	440,250	409,489	344,115
Manhattan	184,546	117,740	88,074	61,451
Percentage	47.2	26.7	21.5	17.9
Bronx	39,519	67,732	71,903	62,407
Percentage	10.1	15.4	17.6	18.1
Queens	19,794	50,307	55,011	56,599
Percentage	5.1	11.4	13.4	16.4
Richmond	8,728	11,036	10,799	9,931
Percentage	2.2	2.5	2.6	2.9
Brooklyn	138,245	193,435	183,702	153,727
Percentage	35.4	43.9	44.9	44.7

Sources: United States Government, U.S. Bureau of the Census, *The Fourteenth Census*, 1920, Vol. II, *Population* (Washington, D.C.: Government Printing House, 1922), 730; *The Fifteenth Census, 1930*, Vol. II, *Population*, 301; *The Sixteenth Census*, 1940, Vol. II, *Population*, 166, 173, 180, 187, 194; *1950 United States Census of Population*, Bulletin, D-37, *New York, N.Y.*, 9, 34, 85, 101, 141.

over 90 percent of the New York Chinese were laundrymen.[35] As mentioned in chapter 3, in 1930 nearly 61 percent of the gainfully employed New York Chinese worked in the laundries and restaurants. These Asian immigrants remained economically marginalized until after World War II.[36] As our earlier discussion suggests, factories could concentrate in a given area and ignore being close to customers; their immediate need was workers.[37] In the mid-1880s, for example, most of the three hundred Chinese cigarmakers lived in the Chinatown area. Mig Atak's factory, the biggest Chinese cigar manufacturer in New York, which hired twenty-five to one hundred workers then, located at 91 Chatham Street. Sam You and Hong Kee Kang—the Civil War veteran—opened their factories at 495 Chatham and 500 Pearl respectively.[38] But, for the Chinese in the laundry industry, proximity to customers must have weighed heavily when they were deciding where to open their firms.[39] "The biggest taboo for Chinese laundries and restaurants," observed a New York Chinese newspaper in 1953, "is for them to cluster in one given area, which means cut-throat competition for business. . . . Therefore, the New York Chinese prefer not to concentrate [in Chinatown]."[40] Since the number of Chinese laundrymen increased over the years (from 4,500 in 1885 to 8,000 in 1898, and again to more than 10,000 by 1933),[41] it comes as no surprise that Chinese laundries dispersed around the city to better thrive or, at least, to survive.

In the late 1880s, "nearly every street and avenue in New York became filled with Chinese laundries," according to a contemporary New York Chinese.[42] The trend of dispersal continued in the following decade. In 1898, Louis Beck, a journalist, remarked, "The thousands of [Chinese] laundrymen scattered through the Metropolis."[43] Chinese laundries must have scattered quite widely by the early twentieth century, otherwise attacking Chinese laundries could not have become "a form of amusement very popular in certain quarters" of New York City, as the *New York Tribune* reported.[44] Immigrants' memoirs and historical novels also provided abundant examples of Chinese laundrymen working outside Chinatown during the 1930s and 1940s. Lee Gong, a main figure in Chu's *Eat a Bowl of Tea*, worked in a laundry in the Bronx in the 1930s.[45] When Sin Jang Leung first arrived in New York in 1938, he stayed at his uncle's laundry on 170th Street and Broadway. Later, he worked at a laundry on 82nd Street. During the 1940s, he first labored at a shirt press shop on Jerome Avenue and then in a laundry in Jackson Heights, both outside Chinatown.[46] In his autobiography, Leung observes that "They [New York Chinese laundrymen] worked year in and year out in a laundry. . . . They wouldn't step out of the laundry. If they ever went to Chinatown, they would just shop for food to last them for the rest of the week."[47] This is a clear indication that most New York Chinese laundrymen lived in white neighborhoods in the 1930s and 1940s.

As we read Leung, we should also remember that Chinese laundrymen usually worked very long hours, often until, even after, midnight.[48] It was inconvenient and even hazardous to walk home in Chinatown so late, because of whites' violence. This menace probably made most Chinese laundrymen hesitate to establish homes far away from their workplaces. Beck discovered in 1898 that Chinese laundrymen lived in "the bachelor quarters in the vicinities where they labor[ed]."[49] Sin Jang Leung walked a few bus stops to work in the 1930s and early 1940s.[50] In a way Chinese thriftiness worked to the same effect as white violence. Most Chinese immigrants wished to return to their native villages in China to become small landowners, so they tried to save money. Because the Chinese Exclusion Act forbade Chinese women to join their husbands, New York's Chinese workers were effectively single. It was therefore both practical and economical for the laundrymen to spend the night in their laundries. And, for decades before the 1960s, many of them indeed did.[51] *Harper's Weekly* reported in 1888:

> A very large majority of the Chinamen in the neighborhood of New York live in boarding houses at a cost which to an American would seem insignificant. . . . It is a common thing for Chinese merchants to keep boarding houses for their employes [*sic*] in the same building with their

stores . . . for the Chinese know no eight-hour law, as may easily be noted at any of their laundries, where work never ceases as long as there is anything to be done.[52]

Thus when Chinese laundries gradually scattered, so did their staff's abodes.

The situations of Chinese restaurants and other businesses, as shown in table 4.3, reinforce the point that the kind of customers they wanted to serve often determined their locations and the workplaces of their staff.

Obviously, businesses mainly catering to the Chinese community, such as groceries and meat stores, almost all located in Chinatown and its vicinity to be near their customers. Wang Chuck Ting, an elite immigrant in Chu's *Eat a Bowl of Tea*, owned a drug store and two restaurants. He located the drug store in Chinatown, the two restaurants in white neighborhoods.[53] For immigrants working in the Chinatown firms, living in the enclave meant proximity to their workplaces and fellow countrymen, and enabled them to avoid discrimination.

Table 4.3. Chinese Business Activities in New York City, 1918

Business Type	Location	
	Chinatown & Vicinity	Outside Chinatown
Bakers	3	-
Carpenters	3	-
Cigarmakers	5	1
Doctors	8	1
Drug stores	15	-
Editors	5	-
Electricians	2	-
Fruit stands	5	-
Grocery stores	29	-
Jewelry stores	3	-
Laundry supplies	5	1
Machine shops	6	-
Meat stores	11	-
Noodle makers	4	-
Novelty stores	11	-
Poultry stores	2	-
Restaurants	24	33
Restaurants supplies	5	-
Tailors	6	-
Typesetters	7	-

Source: *Who's Who of the Chinese in New York*, ed. Warner M. Von Norden (New York: n. p., 1918), 86-90.

For all that, Chinese restaurateurs, like laundry owners, needed to cater to a large non-Chinese population as well as to their compatriots. Restaurants that concentrated heavily in Chinatown would not only exacerbate competition among Chinese but be inaccessible to white customers. Therefore, despite harsh discrimination and harassment, more than half of the Chinese restaurants were located outside Chinatown in the late 1910s.[54] In sum, the need for economic survival outweighed the concern for avoiding racial hostility. As time went by, more Chinese restaurants opened outside Chinatown. In 1958, for example, Times Square alone claimed almost thirty Chinese restaurants.[55] In 1960, of the six hundred Chinese restaurants in Greater New York, only fifty were in Chinatown proper.[56] Understandably, many Chinese immigrants working in a restaurant in a white neighborhood also lived there.

The foregoing discussion, of course, does not imply that the New York Chinese never changed their residences. In fact, many laundrymen and restaurant workers often had to move because small firms frequently went bankrupt. Sin Jang Leung, for example, changed his address at least four times between the late 1930s and 1950s. Moves from one white vicinity to another did not fundamentally alter the overall picture in which, before the 1960s, more and more Chinese chose to live outside Chinatown. One might assume that World War II, which brought so much improvement to the Chinese American community, should also have drastically transformed the residential patterns of the New York Chinese. One should not!

The war and its consequences did bring changes to the residential patterns of the New York Chinese. Among other things, the repeal of the Chinese Exclusion Act in 1943 enabled these Asian immigrants to become U.S. citizens and to send for their wives. The New York Chinese thus began to shift from a bachelor society to an increasingly settled community. At the same time, the vacancy left by the many white men who were drafted into the military meant that Chinese, for the first time, had a chance to work in mainstream factories.[57]

All these changes seemed to signal the beginning of residential as well as social mobility for the New York Chinese. For example, after the war, some second generation Chinese, including a number of ex-servicemen, for the first time in history found mainstream white-collar jobs. With income better than their fathers', quite a few younger Chinese Americans set up their homes in the suburbs of New York.[58] These younger New York Chinese chose to live outside Chinatown for better housing, not necessarily to be close to work.[59] In addition, several thousand Chinese students were stranded in the United States after the Civil War in China (1946-1949). Some of them formed an uptown Chinese population around Columbia University in the early 1950s. These shifts undoubtedly helped swell the proportion of the non-Chinatown Chinese. For several reasons, to predict drastic changes in the residential patterns of the first generation New York Chinese would be simplistic.

First of all, the improvement World War II brought the Chinese community was not without relapses. As mentioned earlier, although many Chinese had an opportunity to work in factories during the war, the majority of them returned to the laundry and restaurant businesses once white workers were discharged from the military.[60] Even by the mid-1950s, most New York Chinese still made their living by laundering.[61] Not surprisingly, the majority of New York Chinese continued to live outside Chinatown then. According to a *New York Times* estimate of 1955, Chinatown in that year had between 5,000 and 7,000 Chinese residents, while about 25,000 New York Chinese lived outside the enclave.[62] A 1954 New York Chinese newspaper explained why most Chinese still lived outside Chinatown in the mid-1950s:

> A special characteristic of the New York Chinese community is that the Chinese widely scatter. They work in the laundries and restaurants all over the five boroughs of New York—Manhattan, Brooklyn, the Bronx, Queens, and Richmond. Because Chinatown is far away, most New York Chinese live in those areas [where they work], widely scattering. Therefore, we see very few fellow Chinese in Chinatown from Monday through Friday. Chinatown appears very quiet and its markets look very desolate on weekdays.[63]

The impact of the workplace also helps us understand the different residential patterns of the Chinese in New York and in other cities. We know that for many years San Francisco's Chinese were more concentrated in Chinatown than their New York counterparts.[64] Of the 521 San Francisco Chinese families interviewed in 1910, all but 21 lived in Chinatown. In the early 1930s, nearly all San Francisco Chinese lived in Chinatown.[65] While 17 percent of New York Chinese resided in Chinatown in 1950, San Francisco's Chinatown housed 70 percent of the city's Chinese in that year.[66]

This disparity was most likely the result of the different occupational situations of the Chinese in the two cities, with the harsher discrimination the Chinese had suffered in California as an original cause. Unlike the New York Chinese, who from the very beginning could only work in the laundry and restaurant industries, the Chinese in San Francisco engaged in a variety of manufacturing occupations in the late nineteenth century. In 1880, for example, more than 28 percent of the Chinatown Chinese in San Francisco worked in the shoemaking, cigarmaking, and clothing factories.[67] Even by the early twentieth century when the anti-Chinese movement had effectively reduced the number of the San Francisco Chinese in manufacturing, the proportion of Chinese in cigarmaking, shoemaking, and clothing factories was still much higher than that of the New York Chinese.[68] The Chinese garment factories in San Francisco had come into existence as early as the 1870s and became a leading industry in Chinatown in the early 1930s.[69] Because factories can concentrate in one area, many San Francisco Chinese were able to work and to live in Chinatown. A 1953 New York Chinese newspaper explains why the Chinese in the two cities followed different residential patterns:

> The New York Chinese are different from their counterparts in other towns. In cities such as San Francisco, the Chinese concentrate in the Chinatown area. But in New York, for occupational reasons, the Chinese widely scatter. In New York, most Chinese engage in the laundry and restaurant businesses. Concentration of laundries and restaurants in one given area is the biggest taboo for these firms. Therefore, the Chinese in this city do not like to cluster [in Chinatown].[70]

Other Chinese American communities, though much smaller than New York's or San Francisco's, also testify to the importance of the workplace in affecting immigrants' residential location choices. Like the New York Chinese in the 1870s, most Chinese in Chicago concentrated in Chinatown in the 1880s.[71] They began to disperse at the end of that decade, and by 1890, Chinese were found in all but two of the 34 wards in the city. While there were only 567 Chinese in Chicago in 1890, 19 wards had 10 or more Chinese each.[72] In 1934, the approximately 2,500 Chinese were found in all but 3 of the 116 census tracts in Chicago with 15 tracts each having 10 or more Chinese and 98 each having less than 10.[73] The scattering of the Chicago Chinese was due to the range of their workplaces: Most Chicago Chinese engaged in the laundry and restaurant businesses and needed to cover a wide area to serve their customers. According to a 1926 study of the Chicago Chinese, a total 67 Chinese restaurants and 45 Chinese laundries located on 47 different streets all over Chicago.[74] Table 4.4 illustrates the spread of Chinese laundries and restaurants in Chicago in 1951.

The residential pattern of the Boston Chinese, on the other hand, seemed to more closely resemble that of the Chinese in San Francisco. From 1890 through 1950, approximately 80 percent of Boston Chinese lived in Chinatown.[75] According to the *Chinese Directory of Boston and New England* published in 1949, of the 2,500 Boston Chinese, 2,000 lived in Chinatown. The other 500, representing nearly all who worked in the laundries and restaurants outside Chinatown, resided in white neighborhoods.[76] As table 4.5 shows, in 1949, of Boston's 112 Chinese laundries and restaurants, well over two-thirds were outside Chinatown but not one of the other 47 Boston businesses then run by Chinese was outside Chinatown.

Why did such a large group of Chinese live in Chinatown while most Chinese laundries and restaurants were located in the white neighborhoods? This question is not difficult to answer. From table 4.5, we can see clearly that, in comparison with laundries and restaurants, the Boston Chinese had nearly half as many trading companies or grocery stores located in Chinatown. Perhaps these Chinatown firms hired more people than the laundries or restaurants. Secondly, and more importantly, an increasing number of garment factories were established in Boston's Chinatown during the 1930s and 1940s. These Chinatown garment factories employed nearly all the adult Chinese women in Boston.[77] According to a contemporary estimate, approximately eight hundred

Table 4.4. Distribution of Chinese Businesses in Chicago, 1951

	Chinatown	North Side	West Side	South Side	Total
Laundries	3	127	132	168	430
Restaurants	14	69	29	55	167
Grocery store & Associations	98	6	13	1	118

Source: *Chicago Chinese Directory*, 1951, cited in Liang, "The Chinese Family in Chicago" (master's thesis, University of Chicago, 1951), 23.

Table 4.5. Locations of Chinese Businesses in Boston, 1949

	in Chinatown	outside Chinatown
Laundries	4	48
Restaurants	26	34
Trading companies & grocery stores	43	0
Others	4	0

Source: *Chinese Directory of Boston and New England*, 1949, cited in Rhoads Murphey, "Boston's Chinatown," 252.

Chinese women came to Boston between 1940 and 1950.[78] From this estimate, we can reasonably infer that several hundred Chinese women worked in the garment factories in Boston's Chinatown. The garment factories plus the relatively large number of trading companies and grocery stores explain why Boston's Chinese were concentrated in Chinatown.

In sum, Chinese immigrants in the United States participated in two different types of ethnic economies. In San Francisco and Boston, many Chinese worked in the garment industry, which represented an ethnic enclave economy. But the New York and Chicago Chinese predominantly engaged in small businesses such as laundries and restaurants. In San Francisco and Boston, an enclave economy resulted in the clustering of Chinese in Chinatown. Concentration in small businesses, on the other hand, was responsible for the scattering of the Chinese in New York and Chicago.

The different types of ethnic economy most likely resulted from the varied demographic as well as economic structures of the cities in which Chinese had settled. For many years, Chinese immigrants were a substantial minority in San Francisco. Although by the end of the nineteenth century many Chinese there had been driven out of the mainstream economy, their relatively large number guaranteed a constant demand for Chinese goods and a sizable ethnic labor pool, both favored the emergence of an ethnic enclave economy. On the other hand, Chinese were latecomers in New York where large numbers of European immigrants had dominated all the major industries. The factories, moreover, were concentrated in areas inhabited by recent European immigrants. The only economic niches left for the Chinese, a small minority, were laundries and restaurants.

Although many New York Chinese had to live outside Chinatown to be close to their workplaces, discrimination and harassment remained significant in immigrants' lives. Because there was scant possibility of socializing with their white neighbors, it almost became a rule for Chinese laundrymen and restaurant workers to spend their days off in Chinatown.[79] In this almost homogeneous enclave, they could shop for Chinese food, play games with fellow townsmen or kinsmen, and, above all, be recognized as human beings.[80] Consequently, until the 1980s, nearly all Chinese grocery stores and social organizations were in Chinatown proper.[81]

The continued existence of Chinatown contrasted sharply with the decline of the Little Italys. The Italians' movement out of Manhattan after World War I led to their ethnic localities' rapid decline.[82] It is true that, in the wake of Italians' migration out of lower Manhattan, some new Italian neighborhoods emerged in Queens and Brooklyn, but for segregation from the larger society these new ethnic neighborhoods did not compare with Chinatown. For example, Italian social organizations no longer concentrated in these neighborhoods; they became widespread.[83] In contrast, even by the 1980s, nearly all the New York Chinese social organizations remained in Manhattan's Chinatown.[84]

The movement of the New York Chinese was not always out of Chinatown. The proportion of Chinese living in Chinatown actually began to rise after the mid-1950s until it reached 43.5 percent in 1960 and nearly 50 percent in 1970, compared with the 1950 record of 17.4 percent.[85] In 1980, Manhattan's Chinatown and a new Chinese enclave in Queens housed about 52 percent of New York City's Chinese.[86] It appears strange then that, with the crumbling of racial discrimination after the early 1960s, more and more Chinese took up residence in Chinatown(s) instead of settling elsewhere. To understand this issue we have to remember that the increase in Chinatown's population after the early 1960s came mainly from two distinct groups.

The 1960s saw the decline of Chinese laundries as a result of the retirement of many laundrymen and the purchase of washing machines by American families.[87] At the same time, better housing available in Chinatown attracted many laundrymen to settle there, close to a familiar culture. A survey conducted in 1968 informs us that a majority of the 565 interviewees resided in Chinatown because of the common culture there.[88] Again, those who went back to China to marry after World War II began to think about getting good educations for their children, who had become teenagers by the 1960s. As a *New York Times* report of 1967 observed:

> Members of other immigrant groups have succeeded in breaking away from their ghettos and so have some Chinese. But some Chinese-American families are now moving back to Chinatown from as far away as New Jersey as better housing becomes available. One such favored development is Chatham Towers, a high-rise project on Park Row.

Chinatown's schools are another attraction for these returning families.[89]

While for those older immigrants who had moved to Chinatown in the 1960s, a familiar culture, better housing, and children's education might have become more important than living close to work, for newcomers who arrived in New York after 1965, avoiding lengthy commutes still weighed heavily when they decided where to live.

The year 1965 witnessed the passage of the most liberal immigration act in American history. Large numbers of Chinese immigrants, together with those from other countries, began to arrive in New York after 1965. These newcomers often chose Chinatown to live because of the lower rent there and because of the language barriers outside.[90] Almost at the same time, and probably not coincidentally, concentration in small businesses began to give way to an ethnic enclave economy characterized especially by the rise of the Chinese garment industry in New York. In the late 1950s, New York City only claimed about a dozen Chinese garment factories.[91] The number of such firms had grown to forty by the mid-1960s and to about five hundred by the early 1980s.[92] Realizing that the newcomers could not afford to leave Chinatown, and that they could hardly find workers elsewhere willing to accept low wages, most employers located their garment factories in Chinatown to be near their potential workers.[93] Indeed, these garment factories absorbed an overwhelming majority of the immigrant Chinese women who resided in Chinatown and its vicinity.[94] Factories moving to be nearer the workers did not alter the situation from the pre-1965 arrangement where workers chose residents near their work—both reflected the immigrants' preference for living close to their work.

Moreover, Chinatown after the early 1960s had increasingly become a tourist attraction. This encouraged the establishment of many Chinese restaurants and curio shops there. The garment factories further stimulated the establishment of new Chinese restaurants in Chinatown as the seamstresses often needed to buy food after a day's busy work.[95] Understandably, the willingness of large numbers of restaurant workers to live near their workplaces also contributed to the concentration of Chinese in Chinatown after the 1960s. Table 4.6, based on New York Chinatown Study Group's report of 1969, corroborates our argument. Not considering the students, housewives, and the non-applicable group, the three largest groups were garment and restaurant workers and the retired.

The trend of concentrating in Chinatown was further strengthened by the arrival of thousands of undocumented immigrants from Fuzhou, south China, in the mid-1980s. Even more reluctant to leave the Chinese enclave than the legal immigrants, most of these Fuzhounese found work in the Chinatown garment factories or restaurants.[96] The overcrowding of Manhattan's Chinatown gave rise in the 1980s to two new Chinatowns in New York City, one in Flushing, Queens, and the other in Sunset Park, Brooklyn. The establishment of new Chinatowns, however, is arguably better understood as the extended, if

Table 4.6. Occupations of the Interviewees Living in New York Chinatown, 1968

Occupation	Number	Percentage
Unemployed	58	2.9
Restaurant personnel	252	12.7
Laundry personnel	67	3.4
Garment factory personnel	234	11.8
Other unskilled labor	73	3.7
Semi-skilled labor	60	3.0
Professional labor	19	1.0
Students	553	27.9
Housewives	183	9.2
Retired	143	7.2
Non-applicable	337	17.0

Source: New York Chinatown Study Group, *Chinatown Report 1969* (New York, n. p., 1970), 18.

distributed, concentration of Chinese in their ethnic enclaves than as their dispersal.

II

With the impact of the location of workplaces becoming clear, we can now examine Chinese immigrants' residential patterns from a broader perspective. Apparently, four forces affected immigrants' decisions on where to live. Three—a familiar culture, housing discrimination, and harassment from white neighbors—tended to push the Chinese toward Chinatown. The other force—the immigrants' wish to live close to their workplaces—often drew them from the enclave. From the 1880s to the 1950s, the force pulling the New York Chinese out of Chinatown was on the whole more powerful than the ones pushing them toward it. The stronger force that pulled the Chinese out of Chinatown was the result of their employment concentration in the laundry and restaurant industries before the 1960s. In sum, concentration in small business led to residential dispersal.

The impact of the workplace in determining immigrants' residential patterns also explains why Chinese immigrants in America followed different residential models in different cities. Whether or not a Chinese firm needed to be close to its customers was the key. In New York City and Chicago, Chinese immigrants lived in widely scattered areas due to their employment concentration in small Chinese businesses whose survival depended on their proximity to customers. By contrast, an ethnic enclave economy, which did not need to be close to its customers, led the San Francisco and Boston Chinese, and the Chinese in post-1965 New York City, to concentrate in Chinatown.

Although this chapter emphasizes the crucial role of workplaces in affecting immigrants' residential location choices, it does not view the ethnic economy as an exclusive force at work. Instead, it reveals a complicated relationship between the various forces affecting immigrants' residential choices. Scholars of the economic sociology of immigration perceive immigrants as rational actors "pursuing goals through deliberately selected means."[97] The New York Chinese were obviously rational actors who had compared the two choices before them—avoiding discrimination or living close to work—and concluded that making a living was even more crucial than avoiding discrimination and harassment. This explains why the great majority of them lived in white neighborhoods before the mid-1960s.

Notes

1. Min Zhou, for example, has observed in her study of New York's Chinatown that "before 1965, most of the Chinese immigrants were concentrated in Manhattan's Chinatown." See Zhou, *Chinatown: The Socioeconomic Potential of an Urban Enclave*, 186; see also Yuan, "Voluntary Segregation: A Study of New York Chinatown," 255.

2. D.Y. Yuan, "Voluntary Segregation: A Study of New York Chinatown," 260-61.

3. Lau, "Traditionalism and Change in a Chinese American Community," 116. So far there is only one sociological study that deals tangentially with the relationship between the New York Chinese residential patterns and their workplaces. But the study only focuses on the post-1970 New York Chinatown and, as the authors point out, they are "not really interested in where people live or work, or what industry they are employed in." See Min Zhou and John R. Logan, "Returns on Human Capital in Ethnic Enclaves: New York City's Chinatown," *American Sociological Review*, 54 (October 1989), 809-20, especially 811.

4. Louis Beck, *New York's Chinatown*, 11. See also Betty Lee Sung, *The Adjustment Experience of Chinese Immigrant Children in New York City* (New York: Center for Migration Studies, 1987), 34.

5. Lan Bin Chen, "Shi Mei Ji Lue (A Brief Record of My Mission to the United States)," in *Xiao Fang Hu Zhai Yu Di Cong Chao (A Collection of Studies of Geography from Xiao Fang Hu Study)*, Vol. 12, 74. Chen was the first Chinese minister to the United States. He passed New York City in 1878 on his way to Washington, D.C. See also Tchen, "New York Chinese," 161-62.

6. In 1880, there were only 747 Chinese immigrants living in New York City. But by 1890 the number of Chinese in New York had reached 2,048. *The Tenth Census, 1880*, 422, and *The Eleventh Census*, 1890, 646.

7. Wong Chin Foo, "The Chinese in New York," 300.

8. *Harper's Weekly*, 1 December 1888, 918; see also Tchen, *New York Before Chinatown*, 236-37.

9. *New York Times*, 30 May 1869.

82 Chapter 4

10. *New York Sun*, 7 March 1880, cited in Bonner, *Alas!* 46.
11. *New York Times*, 7 May 1881 and *New York Tribune*, 7 May 1881, cited in Bonner, *Alas!* 122.
12. *New York Tribune*, 31 July 1900.
13. *New York Tribune*, 27 September 1901.
14. *New York Times*, 21 March 1890.
15. *New York Times*, 21 March 1890. No report was made on the result of this campaign.
16. *New York Tribune*, 23 January 1898.
17. *Wei Xin Bao*, 6 September 1922; *Guo Quan Bao*, 20 December 1931 and 5 June 1932.
18. Gwen Kinkead, "A Reporter At Large: Chinatown," *The New Yorker*, 10 June 1991, 81.
19. See Sin Jang Leung's autobiography, "A Laundryman Sings the Blues," translated by Marlon K. Hom, *Chinese America: History and Perspectives* (1991), 15. For more information on the harassment against Chinese immigrants in white neighborhoods, see Joan Faung Jean Lee, *Asian Americans: Oral Histories of First to Fourth Generation Americans from China, the Philippines, Japan, India, the Pacific Islands, Vietnam and Cambodia* (New York: New Press, 1992), 6-7.
20. Gilbert Osofsky, *Harlem: The Making of a Ghetto, Negro New York, 1890-1930*, second edition (Chicago: Ivan R. Dee Publisher, 1996), 105-07.
21. Osofsky, *Harlem*, 130-31.
22. Allan H. Spear, *Black Chicago: The Making of a Negro Ghetto, 1890-1920* (Chicago: University of Chicago Press, 1967), 11, 20-22. For information on the formation of black ghettos in Philadelphia, see Vincent P. Franklin, "The Philadelphia Race Riot of 1918," in *Black Communities and Urban Development in America, 1720-1990*, ed. Kenneth L. Kusmer, Vol. 5, *The Great Migration and After, 1917-1930* (New York: Garland, 1991), 20-24, 31; and Fredric Miller, "The Black Migration to Philadelphia: A 1924 Profile," *Black Communities and Urban Development in America*, Vol. 5, 82-85.
23. According to police inspector Nicholas Brooks in charge of the Chinatown area in 1898, most New York Chinese lived in the area surrounded by Pell, Mott, and Doyers Streets. See Beck, *New York's Chinatown*, appendix, 324. When he visited New York's Chinatown in 1902, Prince Ts'ai Chen of China advised the residents there to "move out of here and mix more with the people." This report suggests that in the beginning of the twentieth century, many New York Chinese still concentrated in the Chinatown area. See *New York Times*, 13 August 1902.
24. In fact, nationwide discrimination against Chinese Americans in housing lasted into the 1950s. *New York Times*, 17 and 19 February 1952 and 9 July 1959; see also S. W. Kung, *Chinese in American Life: Some Aspects of their History, Status, Problems and Contributions* (Westport, Conn.: Greenwood Press, 1962), 171-72; Sung, *Mountain of Gold*, 249; Stanford Lyman, *Chinese Americans* (New York: Random House, 1974), 147-49. Davis McEntire, *Residence and Race: Final and Comprehensive Report to the Commission on Race and Housing* (Berkeley: University of California Press, 1960), 2.
25. Marie Concistré, "A Study of a Decade in the Life and Education of the Adult Immigrant Community in East Harlem, New York City" (Ph.D. dissertation, New York

University, 1943), in *The Italians*, ed. Cordasco and Bucchioni, 235.

26. Salvatore John LaGumina, *The Immigrants Speak: Italian Americans Tell Their Story* (New York: Center for Migration Studies, 1981), 130-31.

27. Danna Gabaccia, "Little Italy's Decline: Immigrant Renters and Investors in a Changing City," in *The Landscape of Modernity: Essays on New York City, 1900-1940*, ed. David Ward and Olivier Zunz (New York: Russell Sage Foundation, 1992) 240-41.

28. Samuel Bailey, "The Adjustment of Italian Immigrants in Buenos Aires and New York, 1870-1914," *The American Historical Review*, Vol. 88, No. 2 (1983), 288, 291.

29. Edward E. Pratt, "Industrial Causes of Congestion of Population, New York City" (Ph.D. dissertation, Columbia University, 1911), 138-40.

30. Donna Gabaccia, *From Sicily to Elizabeth Street: Housing and Social Change among Italian Immigrants, 1880-1930* (Albany, N.Y.: State University of New York Press, 1984), 78.

31. Gabaccia, *From Sicily to Elizabeth Street*, 66.

32. Nancy L. Green, "Sweatshop Migration: The Garment Industry between Home and Shop," *The Landscape of Modernity*, ed. Ward and Zunz, 220; Selma C. Berrol, *East Side/East End: Eastern European Jews in London and New York, 1870-1920* (New York: Praeger, 1994), 118.

33. Deborah Dash Moore, "On the Fringes of the City: Jewish Neighborhoods in Three Boroughs," in *The Landscape of Modernity*, ed. Ward and Zunz, 257-58.

34. Moore, "On the Fringes of the City," 255; Berrol, *East Side/East End*, 133.

35. According to an 1885 report, there were 4,500 laundrymen among the New York Chinese while artisans, merchants, and other workers numbered just a few hundred; see *New York Tribune*, 21 June 1885. A Chinese American journalist pointed out in 1888 that over 90 percent of the New York Chinese were in the laundry industry. See Wong Chin Foo, "The Chinese in the United States," *Chautauquan*, October 1888 to July 1889, 215-217, cited in Renqiu Yu, *To Save China, To Save Ourselves: A History of the Chinese Hand Laundry Alliance of New York City* (Philadelphia: Temple University Press, 1992), 207. For a contemporary discussion of why most New York Chinese ended up doing laundering, see Wong Chin Foo, "The Chinese in New York," 298.

36. The 1930 census indicates that close to 61 percent of the gainfully employed Chinese in New York State worked in restaurants or laundries. Since at that time most New York State Chinese resided in New York City, the proportion for the city must be fairly close to that for the state. See United States Government, U.S. Bureau of the Census, *The Fifteenth Census, 1930*, Vol. V, *General Report on Occupations* (Washington, D.C.: Government Printing House, 1931), 95-97.

37. Consider, for example, the Chinese garment industry, which had become a leading economic pursuit among the New York Chinese since the 1960s. Until the early 1980s, the overwhelming majority of these clothing factories had located in Chinatown and its vicinity. *The New York Chinese Business Directory* of 1984 enumerated 425 Chinese garment factories, of which 422, or 99 percent, located in Chinatown and its immediate vicinity. See *The New York Chinese Business Directory* (New York: Key Advertising Ent. Inc., 1984), 319-45.

38. *New York Tribune*, 24 July 1882, cited in Bonner, *Alas!* 67.

39. See William K. Tai, *Niu Yue Hua Qiao She Hui (The Chinese Community in New*

York City) (New York: New York Chinese History Research Society, 1950), 17.

40. *Mei Zhou Hua Qiao Ri Bao*, 21 December 1953.

41. Many sources suggest that the number of Chinese laundrymen in New York increased over the years except, perhaps, for the 1900s and 1910s when the Chinese Exclusion Act led to a decline in New York's Chinese population. In 1885, 4,500 Chinese worked in the city as laundrymen. See *New York Tribune*, 21 June 1885. By the end of the nineteenth century, the number of New York Chinese laundrymen had jumped to 8,000. See Beck, *New York's Chinatown*, 28. According to a report of the New York City Department of Licenses in 1933, there were between 6,000 and 7,500 Chinese laundries in the city. Considering the fact that some laundries hired 2 to 3 helpers, the number of Chinese laundrymen should be more than 10,000. See City Department of Licenses, *Report for June 30, 1933*, Box 633, Collection of John O'Brien, 1922-33, Municipal Archives, New York, Cited in Renqiu Yu, *To Save China, To Save Ourselves*, 207-8.

42. Wong Chin Foo, "The Chinese in New York," 25.

43. Beck, *New York's Chinatown*, 46.

44. *New York Tribune*, 27 September 1901.

45. Chu, *Eat a Bowl of Tea*, 17.

46. See Leung, "A Laundryman Sings the Blues," 14, 18, 20.

47. Leung, "A Laundryman Sings the Blues," 16.

48. See, for example, Leung's autobiography, "A Laundryman Sings the Blues," 15.

49. Beck, *New York's Chinatown*, 45.

50. Leung, "A Laundryman Sings the Blues," 14.

51. Beck, *New York's Chinatown*, 46; Carl Glick, *Shake Hands with the Dragon* (New York: H. Jenkins, 1946), 189.

52. *Harper's Weekly*, 1 December 1888.

53. Chu, *Eat a Bowl of Tea*, 27.

54. *Who's Who of the Chinese in New York*, ed. Warner M. Von Norden (New York: n. p., 1918), 88-89.

55. See *Mei Zhou Hua Qiao Ri Bao*, 14 April 1958.

56. Kung, *Chinese in American Life*, 181-82.

57. Some construction companies, for example, advertised jobs in New York Chinese newspapers. See, for example, *Xin Bao*, 30 May 1944. By 1942, some Chinese restaurants in New York had to close since many waiters went to work in factories which offered better wages. See Takaki, *Strangers from a Different Shore*, 374.

58. See Peter Kwong, *The New Chinatown* (New York: Hill and Wang, 1987), 71.

59. *New York Times*, 12 January 1947.

60. See Jian Xiong Wu, *Hai Wai Yi Min Yu Hua Ren She Hui*, 267. Wu interviewed quite a few Chinese ex-servicemen in New York City and found that more than half of them had returned to the laundry and restaurant businesses after the war.

61. According to a *Mei Zhou Hua Qiao Ri Bao* report of 1954, more than ten thousand New York Chinese worked in laundries. This was more than half of the New York Chinese population in the mid-1950s. See *Mei Zhou Hua Qiao Ri Bao*, 6 September 1954.

62. *New York Times*, 27 February 1955.

63. *Mei Zhou Hua Chiao Ri Bao*, 6 September 1954.

64. *Mei Zhou Hua Qiao Ri Bao*, 21 December 1953.

65. Yung, *Unbound Feet*, 78-79, 181.

66. Noel P. Gist and Sylvia F. Fava, *Urban Society* (New York: Thomas Y. Crowell Company, 1964), 132. *Mei Zhou Hua Qiao Ri Bao*, 21 December 1953.

67. See John W. Stephens, "A Quantitative History of Chinatown, San Francisco, 1870 and 1880," in *The Life, Influence and the Role of the Chinese in the United States, 1776-1960*, 78.

68. Erica Y.Z. Pan, *The Impact of the 1906 Earthquake on San Francisco's Chinatown* (New York: Peter Lang, 1995), 18, 144.

69. Dean Lan, "Chinatown Sweatshops," in *Counterpoints, Perspectives on Asian America*, ed. Emma Gee (Los Angeles: Asian-American Studies Center, University of California at Los Angeles, 1976), 351-52; Yung, *Unbound Feet*, 88.

70. *Mei Zhou Hua Qiao Ri Bao*, 21 December 1953.

71. See Yuan Liang, "The Chinese Family in Chicago" (master's thesis, University of Chicago, 1951), 23.

72. United States Government, U.S. Bureau of the Census, *The Eleventh Census, 1890*, Vol.1, *Population* (Washington, D.C.: Government Printing House, 1895), Part I, 454-55.

73. Charles S. Newcomb and Richard O. Lang, *Census Data of the City of Chicago, 1934* (Chicago: n.p., 1934), 668, cited in Liang, "The Chinese Family in Chicago," 22.

74. Ting-chiu Fan, "Chinese Residents in Chicago" (master's thesis, University of Chicago, 1926), cited in Liang, "The Chinese Family in Chicago," 22.

75. See Rhoads Murphey, "Boston's Chinatown," *Economic Geography*, Vol. XXVIII, No. 3 (July 1952), 248.

76. Murphey, "Boston's Chinatown," 248, 255.

77. Murphey, "Boston's Chinatown," 252, 254.

78. Murphey, "Boston's Chinatown," 254.

79. See *New York Times*, 27 February 1955.

80. Paul C.P. Siu, *The Chinese Laundryman, A Study of Social Isolation*, ed. John Kuo Wei Tchen (New York: New York University Press, 1987), 137, 145.

81. "List of the Addresses of the Social Organizations of the Chinese in New York City," in *Special Bulletin of the Fifth Anniversary of the Chinese Hand Laundries Association of New York* (New York: n. p., 1938), 91-93; "Chinese Social Organizations of Greater New York," in *Special Bulletin of the 50th Anniversary of the Chinese Chamber of Commerce of New York* (New York: n. p., 1957), 53-57; "List of Chinese Business and Social Organizations in New York City," in *Journal of Chinese-American Restaurant Association* (New York: n. p., 1975), 43-55; and *The New York Chinese Business Directory*, 1984.

82. United States Government, U.S. Bureau of the Census, *The Fourteenth Census, 1920*, Vol. II, *Population* (Washington, D.C.: Government Printing House, 1922), 730; *The Sixteenth Census, 1940*, Vol. II, *Population* (Washington, D.C.: Government Printing House, 1942), Part V, 166, 173, 180, 194; Concistré, "A Study of a Decade in the Life and Education of the Adult Immigrant Community in East Harlem," in *The Italians*, ed. Cordasco and Bucchioni, 233; *New York Times*, 30 May 1966 and 15 October 1968; and Edward Corsi, "Italian Immigrants and their Children," in *The Italians*, ed. Cordasco and Bucchioni, 217.

83. See, for example, Ware, *Greenwich Village*, 157-58.

84. *New York Chinese Business Directory* (1984), 223-30.

85. Kuo, *Social and Political Change in New York's Chinatown*, 5. Some scholars and journalists, however, think that the actual number of Chinese residing in Chinatown proper in the late 1960s was 40,000, which is higher than the census figure. If their estimate is accurate, then the proportion of Chinese living in Manhattan's Chinatown in the late 1960s would be around 50 percent of New York City's Chinese population. See also *New York Times*, 28 June 1967; Robin Wu, "New York's Chinatown: an Overview," *Bridge Magazine*, Vol. 1, No. 1, (1971); and Rocky Chin, "New York Chinatown Today: Community in Crisis," *Amerasia Journal*, No. 1 (1970), 8.

86. In 1980, there were 40,987 Chinese living in Manhattan's Chinatown and about 23,000 in Queen's Chinatown while the total number of Chinese in New York City was 124,764. See New York City, Department of City Planning, *Demographic Profiles: A Portrait of New York City's Community Districts from the 1980 and 1990 Censuses of Population and Housing*, New York, 1992, "Population Characteristics—Manhattan community Districts 2 and 3," 1980 Census STF2 and STF4, 170; see also Hsiang-shui Chen, "Chinese in Chinatown and Flushing," in http://www.qc.edu/Asian_American_ Center/aacre15.html.

87. One estimate in 1977 put the number of New York Chinese laundrymen at 3,000, a sharp decrease from the 1953 record of 10,000. See Kuo, *Social and Political Change in New York's Chinatown*, 47.

88. Because 79 percent of the interviewees had lived in Chinatown for eight or more years, these people belonged to the old immigrants who came to New York before the 1965 Immigration Act went into effect. See New York Chinatown Study Group, *Chinatown Report, 1969* (New York: n. p., 1970), 38.

89. *New York Times*, 28 June 1967.

90. Kwong, *The New Chinatown*, 5, 22.

91. *Mei Zhou Hua Qiao Ri Bao*, 14 April 1958.

92. *Mei Zhou Hua Qiao Ri Bao*, 6 March 1965; Kwong, *The New Chinatown*, 26.

93. In the early 1980s, of the 425 Chinese garment factories in New York, 422, or 99 percent, located in Chinatown and its immediate vicinity. See the *New York Chinese Business Directory* (1984), 319-45. See also Kwong, *The New Chinatown*, 31.

94. Zhou, *Chinatown*, 177.

95. Kwong, *The New Chinatown*, 33.

96. Peter Kwong, *Forbidden Workers: Illegal Chinese Immigrants and American Labor* (New York: New Press, 1997), 20, 116-17.

97. Portes, *The Economic Sociology of Immigration*, 3.

5

Group Loyalties in the Workplace

The issue of group loyalties—allegiance toward one's fellow townsmen and kinsmen instead of toward the whole immigrant community—has not been seriously pursued by students of Chinese American history. Sometimes when a few researchers come close to the subject, they tend only to emphasize the role of Chinese tradition in bringing fellow townsmen and kinsmen together. Virginia Heyer, for example, in her study of the social organizations in New York's Chinatown, has written that

> The social groupings into which the Chinatown people are organized are directly related to the social units they belonged to in China. In China they were members of extended families, villages, *tsu* [lineage], and family-name groups. In New York they belong to village associations, family-name associations, and large territorial associations.[1]

Yvonne M. Lau has similarly observed that "when the Chinese first entered this country 100 years ago, they were quick to establish the type of formal groups known to them in China."[2] This approach, which comes close to seeing group allegiance as an ingrained trait of the Chinese, cannot account for changes in the immigrants' group loyalties. It cannot explain, for example, why group allegiance among the New York Chinese began to decline after the 1950s.

However, some scholars have more usefully stressed the role of legal discrimination and anti-Chinese violence in sustaining Chinese immigrants' group loyalties. In his study of San Francisco's Chinese community, Stanford Lyman has observed:

> Denied naturalization and the franchise for nearly a century, the Chinese, unlike European immigrants, were not the objects of any local ward politicians' solicitations. Left to themselves—except during anti-Chinese campaigns—the Chinese organized their own benevolent, protective, and governmental bodies.[3]

And K. Scott Wong has written that

> While the regional associations may have contributed to the factional
> strife in Chinatown, these men were not necessarily clinging to regional
> and clan loyalties out of a reluctance to accept their roles as "citizens" in a
> democratic society, but were more likely seeking support from each other
> based on the need for protection in a hostile environment and for a source
> of familiarity in a strange land.[4]

This emphasis on anti-Chinese violence and on legal discrimination that, for
example, deprived Chinese immigrants of the right of naturalization and denied
them the privilege of sending for their wives, is correctly placed. But the
approach proves not inclusive enough to explain why the New York Chinese, in
their reaction to severe discrimination, hewed to group loyalties rather than
attempting to achieve long-term community unity.[5] Finally, neither of the two
above-mentioned approaches helps us understand why group allegiance among
the San Francisco Chinese declined sooner than among the New York Chinese.

This chapter examines the group allegiance of the New York Chinese from
a different perspective. By focusing on the situation at the workplace, we will
find that the ethnic economy had a crucial impact on the vicissitudes of Chinese
immigrants' group loyalties. From the 1890s to the 1960s, the small size of
Chinese laundries and restaurants in New York enabled their owners to hire only
their fellow townsmen or kinsmen. It did not give the Chinese an opportunity to
mingle with workers from different regional and kinship backgrounds in the
workplace. Instead, by limiting their social contact only to fellow townsmen and
kinsmen, it served to keep Chinese immigrants' group loyalties strong. After the
1950s when more and more New York Chinese worked in sizeable garment
factories and large restaurants, immigrants of different district origins and with
different kinship ties for the first time had a chance to mingle with each other
and develop a kind of camaraderie in the workplace. A new situation affecting
workplaces led regional and kinship allegiances to decline.

The primary concern of this chapter is how group loyalties divided the New
York Chinese community and retarded the formation of working class
solidarity. Although we often refer to the history and functions of the social
organizations among the New York Chinese to assess the strength of their group
loyalties, this chapter does not represent a thorough examination of those
organizations per se. Nor does it attempt to fully explore the relationships
among these groupings. Moreover, in the interest of brevity, we mainly focus on
regional and kinship groupings in the New York Chinese community. Other
types of organization, such as secret societies, receive only minimal attention.

I

Like other ethnically distinct immigrants, most Chinese who came to the United States during the nineteenth and most of the twentieth centuries were part of what immigration historians often call chain migrations: Fellow townsmen came after fellow townsmen, and relatives followed relatives. Thus in migrating from Guangdong, China, to the United States, the Chinese brought their regional and kinship ties with them. Trapped in a helpless situation in America, these immigrants employed their group loyalties as important guiding principles for mutual aid and for social groupings.

The regional loyalties of the New York Chinese often expressed themselves through the immigrants' district organizations. As early as the 1870s when the New York Chinese community had barely taken shape, people originally from the same region in Guangdong began to establish various district organizations, or *Hui Guans* as the immigrants called them. The year 1872 witnessed the founding of the first district organization in New York's Chinatown, the Heshan Hui Guan, followed by the Taishan-Ningyang Hui Guan, established in 1890.[6] As time went by, more district organizations were founded among the New York Chinese. The major functions of a Hui Guan included providing various kinds of aid for members of its own association. Its office rooms often served as temporary hotels and recreational centers. Assistance also went to members looking for employment or loans.[7]

Among the New York Chinese, as in other Chinese American communities, people with the same surnames also formed family-name associations, or *Gong Suos* for the purpose of mutual aid.[8] The Lee Family Association, founded in 1886, seems to be the oldest Gong Suo among the New York Chinese. Most family-name associations, however, came into existence during the first half of the twentieth century.[9] Although in many cases no blood relationship was involved between the fictive kinsmen, members of a Gong Suo always referred to each other as cousins and felt obligated to assist each other.[10] Louis Chu's historical novel *Eat a Bowl of Tea* provides us with many good examples of fictive kinship at work. Although Wang Chuck Ting and Wang Wah Gay were not related, Chuck Ting regarded the latter as a younger brother because the two shared the same surname and came from the same village. He always provided generous and timely assistance when the younger one was in need.[11] The major functions of Gong Suos were similar to those of Hui Guans.[12] They certainly included providing various kinds of aid for members of their own associations.[13]

Before the 1960s, the crucial function of group allegiance among the New York Chinese was helping fellow townsmen and kinsmen to find employment, as survival always headed the immigrants' agenda. In fact, many Hui Guans had a tradition of guaranteeing the privilege of their members to be employed by businesses owned by fellow townsmen. The General San Yi District Association in its early years even threatened to penalize any members who employed people of non-San Yi origins.[14] When Arthur Wong first arrived in New York in 1930, for example, it was his family-name association that helped him find a job in a restaurant.[15] Sin Jang Leung would have starved if a kinsman had not found employment for him upon his arrival in New York in 1938.[16] Wang Ben Loy, the protagonist in *Eat a Bowl of Tea*, worked for a fictive kinsman and actual fellow townsman in a restaurant after his discharge from military service in the late 1940s. The arrangement was made by his father with the old man's fictive cousin Wang Chuck Ting.[17]

As pointed out in the beginning of this chapter, earlier historiography tended to depict the Hui Guans and Gong Suos among Chinese immigrants as replicas of the district and lineage organizations in southeast China. Undoubtedly, these organizations did evolve on the basis of the kinship and district networks that immigrants brought to the United States. However, failure to refer to the impact of the American environment will make it difficult for us to explain why Gong Suos became so ubiquitous in Chinese American communities while in the old country people seldom formed family-name associations.[18] At the same time, since it tends to regard group allegiance as an ingrained trait of the Chinese, this interpretation cannot account for changes in the group loyalties of Chinese immigrants. Here the Italian experience will again prove revealing because group allegiance also characterized the New York Italians in their early years.

Regional loyalties brought by the immigrants from the Old World, for example, often determined the residential patterns of the Italians in New York City. When Italians first arrived in New York, fellow townsmen tended to reside on the same streets. "Entire villages have been transplanted from Italy to one New York street," observed a contemporary in 1911. "In one street will be found peasants from one Italian village; in the next street the place of origin is different and distinct, and different and distinct are manners, customs, and sympathies."[19] Western Sicilians, for example, claimed Elizabeth Street, while eastern Sicilians took up their residence on Catharine and Monroe Streets. While Mulberry Street became the home of Neapolitans, Bleecker and MacDougal Streets were inhabited by Genoese and northern Italians respectively.[20] This is because in an unfamiliar and helpless environment, the Italians trusted only their fellow townsmen and wanted to live close to them. Leonard Covello, an immigrant from southern Italy, recalls what his father often told him: "With the Aviglianese you are always safe. . . . They are your countrymen, *paesani*. They will always stand by you."[21] Italian mutual aid societies, in fact, were almost entirely based on the identical district origins in Italy. "No outsider can appreciate how very many mutual benefit societies exist in New York's Italian colony," observed a New York Italian in 1903. "Each province, each town, each village has a society of its own."[22] Banking business was also rooted in this regionalism: Italian immigrants in New York preferred to put their savings into a bank run by a fellow townsman even though other banks were financially more solid.[23]

The foregoing discussion does not imply a similarity of expressions of group loyalties between Italian and Chinese immigrants. The Chinese family-name associations had no equals among Italian immigrants and set the two groups' experiences apart. Migration from Italy to the United States tightened bonds between relatives who tended to become neighbors in New York.[24] "When my family first arrived in the United States," one New York Italian reminisced, "we settled on Union Street in Brooklyn, since it was here that our uncles, aunts, relatives, and friends who had preceded us to America lived."[25] In Buffalo, New York, Italian immigrants were more likely to have joint residence with their kin, in contrast to the situation in the *Mezzogiorno*. Relatives often assumed such functions as employment agents and emotional advisors.[26] A similar situation was found among Italians in Providence, Rhode Island, where parents and siblings were either included as part of a household or lived close by in the neighborhood.[27] In spite of these tightened bonds, they never established organizations for people sharing the same family name. Italians in New York also differed from the Chinese in the rapid decline of their group allegiance after World War I.

Although in the Little Italys the tenements and blocks were early distinguished from each other by provincial lines, this means of demarcation faded by the late 1910s. In 1919 an investigator observed:

> In the old Italian neighborhood, as on the west side, Sicilian, Genoese, and Neapolitans may be found in the same house; and their scorn of one another had become tempered with the mild forbearance of dwellers in the same tenement. The social character of the Italian soon induces the woman from Naples to take her homework into the rooms of her Sicilian neighbor, or Teresa from Genoa to ask her foreman to take Maria into his factory, even though Maria comes from Bacilicata.[28]

Greenwich Village testifies especially to the declining significance of regionalism among the Italians in New York. In 1910, 50 percent of the Italian men in this area belonged to one or another of the mutual aid societies based on district origins. In 1920, only 30 percent of them belonged to such organizations; by 1930, the figure had fallen to 10-15 percent.[29]

Group allegiance among Chinese immigrants underwent changes, too. For all their importance in immigrants' daily lives, regional and kinship loyalties among the New York Chinese demonstrated unequivocal signs of decline after the 1950s. For example, of the 565 people interviewed by the New York Chinatown Study Group in 1969, 78 percent had no family members involved in family-name associations' activities. Because 79 percent of the interviewees had lived in Chinatown for eight or more years, these were mostly people who came to New York City before the 1965 Immigration Act went into effect.[30] The decline of group loyalties, therefore, occurred among the older immigrants.

The changes in the group allegiance among the Chinese as well as among the Italians indicate that these loyalties were not ingrained traits, and they prompt us to examine the issue from a broader perspective. This should surely include the impact of racial discrimination against Chinese. Consider, for example, the lack of nuclear families in the Chinese communities as a result of Chinese exclusion. Traditionally, the Confucian moral code forbade women to leave their homes. Chinese immigrants' wives, therefore, remained in China to fulfill their conventional roles such as raising children and looking after their husbands' parents.[31] Exceptions prove the rule and there were always some individuals who defied tradition, or responded to the American environment, by sending for their wives. This was no longer legally possible after 1882 when the Chinese Exclusion Act was passed by Congress.

The Exclusion Act did more than prohibit Chinese laborers from entering the United States. It forbade Chinese women from joining their husbands who were already there.[32] Thus, until the act's repeal in 1943, most Chinese immigrants were men living a bachelor's life. Without their immediate families around, and often assaulted by violence and harassment, the Chinese found themselves lonelier and more helpless than the Italians who could always legally send for family members to join them. This background enables us to understand why Chinese subsequently stretched the meaning of "family" to form surname associations. To a certain extent, this was also true of the grouping of fellow townsmen. After World War II, with racism wavering and with the Chinese Exclusion Act repealed, a growing number of Chinese women joined their husbands in the United States. The increasing presence of wives and children very likely provided another interest for the former bachelors, who before had pursued the activities of the district and surname associations.

The effects of discriminatory laws on the group allegiance of the New York Chinese are more complex than we might initially suppose. Table 5.1 indicates that until the 1910s the majority of Italian immigrants, like Chinese immigrants, did not in great numbers send for their wives, even though they could.

The table suggests that for several decades, New York's Little Italys were largely bachelors' societies. Because these Italians, almost as powerless as, if slightly less isolated than, the Chinese, did not form fictive or formal kin organizations,[33] we probably should not take the lack of women as the only reason explaining the importance of family-name associations among the Chinese. Outside discrimination would encourage, one might suppose, an immigrant group to overcome small-group loyalties and seek community unity.[34] The New York Chinese experience shows that this supposition is not always borne out.

Although group allegiance facilitated the immigrants' adjustment by providing mutual aid, they simultaneously also divided the New York Chinese. The intimacy between fellow townsmen, for example, often entailed rejection of people of different regional origins. "A sort of mutual strangeness and jealousy

Table 5.1. Immigration to the United States from Italy by Sex and Decade, 1871-1910

Period	Total	Number		Percent	
		Male	Female	Male	Female
1871-1880	55,759	41,779	13,980	74.9	25.1
1881-1890	307,309	243,923	63,386	79.4	21.0
1891-1900	651,893	317,023	106,902	75.0	25.2
1901-1910	2,045,877	1,612,996	432,881	78.8	21.2

Source: *Reports of the Immigration Commission*, Vol. 4, *Emigration Conditions in Europe* (Washington, D.C., 1911), 138.

always existed between people of the different Hiens [counties]," observed a contemporary New York Chinese in the late nineteenth century, "and this is carried with them even into America."[35] Perhaps the feud between the *Kejias* and other Cantonese best illustrates the division among Chinese immigrants. Earlier we mentioned that animosity of the *Bendi* people toward the Kejias eventually translated into a bloody war in the Si Yi area in 1854. The enmity between the two groups carried over to the New World. In 1856, a bloody fight between the two groups in California involved 900 Kejias and 1,200 Bendi immigrants.[36] The Kejias, who came to New York later than the Bendi immigrants, found it difficult to open restaurants in Chinatown in the early twentieth century because the Bendis wanted to control the community and tried to squeeze them out. Eventually, the Kejias could only establish their restaurants outside Chinatown.[37]

For many decades, ties of kinship and fictive kinship likewise split the New York Chinese community, as we read in a New York Chinese newspaper of 1946:

> In traditional Chinese immigrant communities, feudalist thought was ex-traordinarily prevalent, the notion of family names was especially in-grained. Although lately this situation has undergone some change, the notion of family names is still predominant. . . . Therefore, we often see people of a large family-name association look down upon those of a small one. . . . There is a proverb in Chinese-American community: Fix your attention on the first word of one's name [i.e., family name].[38]

In Chu's historical novel about the New York Chinese of the late 1940s, we can also find how the Chinese with different family names repulsed each other. Wang Wah Gay, whose daughter-in-law was seduced by Ah Song, cut off the womanizer's left ear in a rage. Ah Song subsequently filed charges against Wah Gay at the fifth precinct police station. The Wangs in New York immediately came to Wah Gay's aid. When they learnt that Ah Song's surname was Jo, the Wangs felt relieved because there were not many Jos around who could help the adulterer. Said a friend to Wah Gay, "Why didn't you kill him? No one will ever miss him. I don't think you can find another Jo in New York." The idea that there were not many Jos around also encouraged Wang Chuck Ting, Wah Gay's fictive cousin and president of the Wang Family Association, to help Wah Gay. Eventually, the Wangs forced Ah Song to withdraw his charges from the police station and to leave New York for five years.[39]

Community disunity certainly was not a unique Chinese characteristic: Regionalism likewise divided the New York Italians in their early years. In the early twentieth century, Manhattan alone had over 150 Italian mutual aid societies based on district origins.[40] Assistance from any society was unavailable for people from different towns. "The moral disunity of the old peninsula is transplanted here," a contemporary observer deplored in 1904. "The Italian does not lack the instinct of charity or mutual helpfulness; but at present he lacks the instinct of charity in a broad sense. He would take the bread from his mouth in order to help his fellow townsmen; there is nothing he will not do for his *paesano*; but it must not be expected from this that he will manifest such an attitude toward all Italians."[41] Another observer who had firsthand experience of living among Italian immigrants on Houston Street also discovered that Italians "of different provinces are constantly arrayed against each other."[42] As mentioned earlier, the divisive effect of Italian regionalism began to decline after World War I.

Among the Italians, furthermore, the decline of regional loyalties coincided with the consolidation of some national organizations. After 1906, for example, more and more mutual-aid societies in New York joined the Order of the Sons of Italy. The Order exerted increasing influence on the Little Italys in the subsequent years.[43] In Chicago, a Sicilian society (*Unione Siciliana*) began to take in various village and regional societies with Sicilian origins after the turn of the century. In later years, the organization continued to expand, not only absorbing Sicilian but also Italian local societies. By 1925, the Unione became a national organization in nature and was renamed the Italo-American National Union by its members. The aim of the renamed society was "closer unity among those of our race into one homogeneous group."[44] Fighting discrimination, which required community-wide unity, was undoubtedly an important reason for the emergence of nation-wide organizations like the Sons of Italy. In a 1926 article entitled "Federation for Mutual-aid Associations," one member of the New York Italian elite observed, "This country's supernationalists have come to look upon the Italian race as inferior and undesirable, and are carrying a legal struggle to overcome us morally and economically. We are all aware of the danger. And we all know that we cannot face the situation individually. . . . We must be strong; therefore we must be united."[45]

A recent study of the social organizations in San Francisco's Chinatown informs us that regional loyalties among the Chinese there quickly dwindled after the early 1910s.[46] By the end of the nineteenth century, the period of

Table 5.2. Chinese District and Surname Organizations Established in New York City, 1910s to 1940s

Year	District and Family Associations
1917	Lei-Fang-Kuang Family Association
1918	Chongzheng Hui Guan
1918	Haiyan Hui Guan
1919	Dapeng Hui Guan
1920	Zhongshan Hui Guan
1920	Panyu Hui Guan
1920	Dongan Hui Guan
1920	Deng-Cen-Ye Family Association
1922	Kaiping Hui Guan
1924	Enping Hui Guan
1926	Chen-Hu-Yuan Family Association
1926	Yu Family Association
1928	Huizhou Hui Guan
1928	Zhu Family Association
1929	Lin Family Association
1929	Jiangsu-Zhejiang-Jianghxi Hui Guan
1934	Nanhai-Shunde Hui Guan
1937	Xinhui Hui Guan
1940	Xue-Situ Family Association
1941	Tan-Tan-Xu-Xie Family Association
1943	Fujian Hui Guan
1947	North China Hui Guan

Sources: Jian-Xiong Wu, *Hai Wai Yi Min Yu Hua Ren She Hui (Chinese Emigration and Overseas Chinese Community)*, 292-96. Data provided by Wu are based on his interview with an ex-president of the Consolidated Chinese Benevolent Association of New York in the early 1990s.

expansion for surname associations in that city had also come to a close. With the decline of regional and kinship loyalties, class confrontation became more important among the San Francisco Chinese.[47] In contrast, many sources suggest that regional and kinship loyalties among the New York Chinese remained strong even after World War II. As table 5.2 illustrates, Hui Guans and Gong Suos were continually established in New York from the late 1910s to the late 1940s.

While reasons for the establishment of new district and family-name organizations could vary, they unmistakably testify to the enduring group loyalties of the older immigrants. Because of their reluctance to assist newcomers from different regional and kinship backgrounds, the new arrivals found no other source of assistance available but an appeal to provincialism and kinship ties in their own ranks.

If the formation of new Hui Guans and Gong Suos did reflect the strength of the immigrants' regional and kinship loyalties, then it appears that group allegiance was especially strong among the New York Chinese during the 1910s and 1920s. These early decades of the twentieth century experienced the arrival of new Chinese immigrants and continued remigration of some California Chinese to New York to avoid the anti-Chinese violence on the West Coast. Because it was difficult to receive help from the old timers, newcomers with different surnames and district origins formed new Hui Guans and Gong Suos. No wonder *Min Qi Ri Bao (The Chinese Nationalist Daily)* drafted an editorial in 1928 strongly urging Chinese immigrants to abandon their regional and kinship loyalties and achieve community unity![48] Since *Min Qi Ri Bao*'s reports almost always centered on the New York Chinese, the editorial clearly indicates that regionalism and kinship loyalties in that community were still strong at least until the late 1920s. Such enduring ties show why kinship and fictive kinship loyalties remained a divisive force among the New York Chinese even until the early 1950s.[49]

It is true that the New York Chinese had a paramount organization, the Consolidated Chinese Benevolent Association (CCBA),[50] which came into existence in 1884 and assumed the functions of a government such as the supervision of business transactions and the settlement of disputes. According to the bylaws of the CCBA, all business transactions had to be reported to the CCBA and taxed.[51] In settling disputes and imposing sanctions, the CCBA's decisions were always final and binding.[52] During the Sino-Japanese War in the late 1930s and early 1940s, the New York Chinese donated generously to their homeland. The few Chinese who refused to make such contributions were summoned to the CCBA's office and told to stand on wooden boxes. Around their necks were hung boards that read, "I am a cold-blooded animal." Each of them was also fined from $65 to $80.[53]

On behalf of the New York Chinese community, the CCBA sometimes took concerted action protesting discrimination from the larger society. In 1954, when some Chinese sailors were in danger of being deported by the Immigration and Naturalization Service, the New York Chinese Sailors Union asked the victims to immediately report the case to the CCBA, which would deal with the U.S. authorities on the sailors' behalf. The CCBA issued a similar notice asking the victims to report themselves to this paramount institution of Chinatown.[54] In the last analysis, the CCBA hardly represented community solidarity. Despite its power, the CCBA's continued efforts to settle disputes between various associations through the 1950s indicate more its failure to suppress the immigrants' small-group loyalties than its success.[55]

The New York Chinese did enjoy a brief period of community unity during World War II when these Asian immigrants felt an urgent need to support their motherland's effort to fight Japanese aggression. Even during this period, regional and kinship loyalties did not disappear from the daily life of the New

York Chinese community. For example, a Tan-Tan-Xu-Xie Gong Suo was formed in 1941.[56] Chinese immigrants with the four surnames had founded a Tan-Tan-Xu-Xie Association in San Francisco in 1896. It was likely that New York City had received quite a few people with these surnames by the early 1940s. Having found the old timers unwilling to help, these new arrivals then could not but form their own Gong Suo for mutual aid. Nevertheless, the war probably did serve to blunt the regional and kinship loyalties of the New York Chinese as indicated by the *China Tribune* in 1946. When the conflict was over, group allegiance remained strong, as the *Tribune* also suggested.[57]

Recently, L. Eve Armentrout Ma has demonstrated that rising nationalism in China in the early twentieth century led to the rapid decline of regionalism in San Francisco's Chinatown. After the aborted 1898 Reform in China,[58] the two foremost reformers, Kang You-wei and his best student Liang Qichao, began to work among overseas Chinese in the hope of reviving the reform. They founded the *Baohuanghui* (Protect the Emperor Society) in North America in 1899. The two leaders' appeal to Chinese immigrants for unity served to permanently blunt the regionalism among the California Chinese.[59]

We know that the influence of Chinese nationalism had also reached New York. The eastern headquarters of the *Baohuanghui* with its six branches and its organ *Wei Xin Bao (Chinese Reform News)* were in New York's Chinatown, and Liang Qichao, who toured New York in 1903, had also broadly contacted the Chinese immigrants there.[60] It appears unlikely that Liang, who strongly urged the San Francisco Chinese to abandon their factionalism based on regional loyalties, failed to persuade the New York Chinese to do the same. Why, faced with severe discrimination and under the same influence of Chinese nationalism, were the New York Chinese so slow in subduing their group allegiance and achieving community unity? Our understanding of this issue will deepen only when we consider the effects of economic discrimination against Chinese. Here, again, a brief review of the Italian experience seems helpful.

Because the overwhelming majority of the New York Italians were factory and construction workers, there seldom existed cutthroat competition for conducting small businesses among these European immigrants. Sometimes, especially during economic recessions, it was difficult to find a job in a factory or on a construction site, to be sure. As we shall see in the following chapter, this difficulty often translated into workers' antagonism toward their employers instead of toward fellow workers even though they were from different towns.

By contrast, economic discrimination resulted in limited resources and opportunities for the New York Chinese. Because working and living in Chinatown would enable the immigrants to avoid outside discrimination and to be close to fellow countrymen, many people must have hoped to do as much business as possible in the enclave. Consequently, restaurants and other businesses in Chinatown became very competitive. This situation was exacerbated by the animosity between immigrants from different regional backgrounds, as we see in the competition between the Kejias and Bendis for opening restaurants in Chinatown. The competitiveness reinforced Chinese immigrants' regional consciousness.

During the early decades of the twentieth century, New York's Chinatown was notorious for its bloody fights—popularly known as *tong* wars—between the secret societies. Although the tong wars were often triggered by more than one factor, competition for the limited resources always constituted the primary motive for the feuds. Tong wars were often intertwined with conflicts between different regional and kinship interests because the tong leaders had infiltrated the Gong Suos and Hui Guans. When they attempted to open restaurants in Chinatown, for example, the Kejia people were repeatedly molested by the tongs whose hatchetmen were Bendis.[61]

District and kinship ties were indispensable for the accumulation of capital among the Chinese. Life was often tough for the unskilled Italian laborers and exchange of favors between kinsmen and neighbors was quite common. Alongside this similarity between Italian and Chinese immigrants' experiences in New York was a contrast. Because family firms never became a dominant business model among the Italians, there existed no economic need for kinsmen to pool their money to start a small business. Among the New York Chinese, however, small businesses such as laundries, restaurants, and grocery stores were always the major places of work. Although to start a small laundry did not require a large sum of money, the amount was beyond the resources of most individual Chinese.[62] Accordingly, kinship ties became a very useful channel for the would-be laundrymen to accumulate capital. In fact, money for small Chinese businesses in New York was almost always pooled among kinsmen. Table 5.3 portrays the situation.

Similarly, Chinese immigrants' workplace tended to perpetuate their group loyalties. It is still not altogether clear why Italian immigrants' regional loyalties began to dwindle within two to three decades of their immigration to New York. Their workplace situations likely hastened the decline. A factory or a

Table 5.3. Sources of Original Capital for 137 Chinese Enterprises in New York City, 1900-1950

Supplied by	Number
Personal Savings	48
Family of Orientation	14
Wui (a kind of informal trust among kinsmen and friends)	55
Kinsmen	12
Chinese Friends	8

Source: Bernard Wong, *A Chinese American Community: Ethnicity and Survival Strategies* (Singapore: Chopmen Enterprises, 1979), 119.

construction site usually hired hundreds, even thousands, of workers, so Italian immigrants often worked shoulder to shoulder with fellow countrymen from different districts. These laborers' role as exploited workers probably provided a more meaningful and evident identity than their Calabrian, Sicilian, or Neapolitan origins. As the previous chapter mentions, with the large-scale migration of Italians from Manhattan after World War I, neighborhood communities rooted in common district origins disintegrated. This undoubtedly contributed to the decline of Italian immigrants' regionalism. The situation of the New York Chinese was very different.

Consider, for example, Chinese laundries in New York. Many Chinese laundries were one-man operated or owned by two or three partners.[63] Those that did need helpers hired four or five people at most.[64] As mentioned earlier, many Hui Guans forbade their members to hire workers of different regional origins. Indeed, the small size of Chinese laundries enabled their owners only to employ their fellow townsmen or kinsmen.[65] Because the overwhelming majority of the New York Chinese kept working in small laundries and restaurants through the 1950s, kinsmen's and fellow townsmen's networks remained important for their finding jobs. The importance of survival thus made it unthinkable for the New York Chinese to dissociate themselves from their Hui Guans and Gong Suos.

As discussed in the previous chapter, many Chinese laundrymen and restaurant workers spent the night in the places where they worked. This means they worked and lived with their fellow townsmen or kinsmen in the same buildings.[66] In *Eat a Bowl of Tea*, for example, we can find that the two fellow townsmen from Xinhui, Wang Ben Loy and Chin Yue, lived in the same apartment while working at a restaurant owned by another fellow townsman.[67] Chinese immigrants, therefore, had little chance to mingle with non-relatives or compatriots from different towns. Chinese employers, furthermore, usually ate and worked with their workers.[68] These juxtapositions plus the extensive use of kinship terms at the workplace created a surrogate family atmosphere, that, in turn, promoted regional and kinship loyalties and hindered the development of class consciousness.[69] The absence of class consciousness was consistent with divided Chinese immigrant workers in New York who staged no strikes against their employers before 1960, as we shall see in chapter 6. Workers who could not achieve industrial solidarity in a single workplace could not hope to reach such unity among all New York Chinese.

If during weekdays the New York Chinese had no chance to overcome their group loyalties, it was not likely that they would do so on the weekend, either. As mentioned in chapter 4, Chinese immigrants living in white vicinities always spent their Sundays in Chinatown because there was no opportunity to socialize with their white neighbors.[70] This did not mean that they socialized with all fellow Chinese there. On the contrary, after shopping for the necessities, they spent the rest of the day in their Hui Guans or Gong Suos with fellow townsmen or fictive kinsmen.[71]

When we keep in mind the effects of economic discrimination, it becomes easier to understand why group loyalties among the New York Chinese weakened after the 1950s. As mentioned earlier, more and more second generation Chinese Americans were able to work in mainstream factories and companies after World War II. Needless to say, these mainstream firms did not operate on Chinese regional and kinship loyalties. Again, we should recall that many Chinese laundrymen retired after the 1950s. This, coupled with the rise of an enclave economy in New York's Chinatown in the 1960s—Chinese garment factories and large Chinese restaurants—further eroded the importance of group allegiance. Although some small clothing factories could continue to hire fellow townsmen and kinsmen, it became difficult for the bigger ones to do so. In fact, a sizable garment factory often employed several dozen people, sometimes even more than a hundred.[72] A large Chinese restaurant, such as Silver Palace, hired more than one hundred workers in the 1980s.[73] The diverse regional back-grounds of the new immigrants added to the difficulty of these large firms' employing only fellow townsmen or kinsmen. Among the Chinese who arrived in the United States after the mid-1960s, some came from Hong Kong, Fujian, Guangdong, and north China.

Within the large garment factories and restaurants, for the first time in many decades unrelated workers, often from different regions, had an opportunity to mingle. Such mingling must have hastened the decline of group allegiances among New York Chinese. Because of the large size of the garment factories and restaurants, bosses and workers no longer worked and ate together. Their separation widened the gap between labor and management. It is likely that many New York Chinese gradually realized, as their Italian counterparts had half a century before, that their role as exploited workers provided a more immediately unifying identity than that of fellow townsmen or fictive kinsmen. As the following chapter shows, class consciousness and working class solidarity began to outweigh regional and kinship loyalties, and Chinatown firms witnessed a series of labor disputes and strikes after the early 1960s.[74]

Class consciousness may also have developed in the smaller garment factories. Although a small clothing factory might continue to employ fellow townsmen or kinsmen, its size—a few dozen workers—was much bigger than a traditional Chinese laundry's, big enough to give space for workers to evolve class consciousness! In her recent study of the immigrant workers in Shanghai, China, in the early twentieth century, Elizabeth J. Perry has argued that although regional loyalties were an important divisive force, they could at the same time promote solidarity among workers within each occupation. This could occur because immigrants from a certain region in China usually concentrated in one particular occupation in Shanghai, and their common heritage was conducive to their unity.[75] The situation in the post-1965 New York Chinese garment factories somehow resembled that in Shanghai described by Perry. Without an evolving class, it is hard to suggest why major Chinese strikes after 1960 attracted workers from the whole Chinese community.[76]

The strike in 1980 by the waiters in Chinatown's largest restaurant, Silver Palace, unquestionably demonstrated for the first time a community-wide working class solidarity. When the waiters walked out and picketed Silver Palace, workers in other Chinese restaurants did not look on with folded arms but gave generously to support the strikers.[77] The 1982 New York Chinese garment workers' strike involved 20,000 seamstresses and presented an even better example of how class consciousness and working-class unity had come to outweigh familial and regional loyalties. During negotiations for a new work contract that would include wage increases for the garment workers, the Chinese contractors refused to take part because white manufacturers left them out of the bargaining. The Chinese contractors appealed to their workers for ethnic unity against racial discrimination. The seamstresses concentrated on economic—not ethnic—themes, insisted on pay increases, and walked out. The turnout of 20,000 people—almost all the garment workers in Chinatown—was unprecedented in New York Chinatown's history. One leader said, "If we cooperate and stand together behind our union, we will win! Let's celebrate our historical show of unity demonstrated today."[78] The newly-emerged working-class solidarity brought the New York Chinese far closer to community unity.

Because these new firms no longer employed solely fellow townsmen or kinsmen, a previously important function of the Hui Guans and Gong Suos—finding employment for members through the regional or kinship networks—dwindled. These functions were increasingly taken up by new organizations, like the Chinatown Planning Council or the Chinatown Youth Council. These organizations were founded in the middle years of the civil rights movement and represented a new approach to the problems that faced Chinese community. Instead of relying on regional or kinship loyalties for mutual aid, the councils sought assistance from, and were funded by, the city and state governments.[79] The executive director of the Chinatown Planning Council reported that it helped several thousand Chinese clients a day in the 1980s—a successful challenge to the traditional organizations![80] This situation understandably accelerated the decline of traditional group allegiance among the New York Chinese.

II

Through our acknowledging the effects of economic discrimination, we now better understand the long-existing dichotomy between order and disunity in the New York Chinese community. Obviously, discrimination against Chinese immigrants had multiple ramifications. While legal discrimination potentially encouraged the Chinese to seek community unity as they had in the concerted actions of the CCBA, everyday realities—like the small size of Chinese laundries and restaurants—had reinforced the immigrants' group allegiance. Before the 1960s, everyday reliance on the regional and kinship loyalties for survival so predominated for the Chinese immigrants that even Chinese nationalism and the need to fight discrimination could only intermittently dissuade the New York Chinese from these loyalties.

Economists and sociologists have addressed, in detail, the effects of segmented work on American workers and concluded that it retarded the formation of a united working class.[81] This chapter argues, however, that the segregation of Chinese immigrants went beyond their apartness from workers of other nationalities. Among the New York Chinese, there was further segmentation due to the small size of their workplaces and its consequences. As a result, for a long time Chinese immigrants could not become part of a united working class, even among themselves.

Finally, if the group loyalties of the New York Chinese indeed remained stronger for longer than those of the Chinese in San Francisco, then economic opportunities, particularly the workplace situation, can help us distinguish and integrate the experiences of the Chinese in both cities. In San Francisco, fewer Chinese worked in laundries, and sizeable Chinese garment factories emerged earlier than in New York. In 1952, for example, San Francisco had about 300 Chinese laundries while even as late as 1958 New York City had 4,000 to 5,000 Chinese laundries.[82] As early as 1873, San Francisco's Chinatown counted 28 Chinese clothing factories, each employing 50 to 100 workers. In 1932, there were at least 30 Chinese garment factories in San Francisco. New York's Chinatown, by contrast, only had about 15 Chinese garment factories in 1958.[83] This means that Chinese immigrants in San Francisco preceded their brethren in New York in mixing with fellow workers from different regional or kinship backgrounds, and in confronting exploitative employers. As we shall see in chapter 6, strikes by Chinese workers against Chinese employers in San Francisco occurred as early as the 1930s, clear evidence of class consciousness and working-class unity outweighing regional and kinship loyalties. The early decline of group loyalties among the San Francisco Chinese, therefore, is an early example of the result of the immigrants' working in an enclave economy—sizeable factories. The example exists alongside the influence of Chinese nationalism in the early twentieth century.

Notes

Part of this chapter appeared in *New York History* (*New York History*, July 1999, Vol. 80, No. 3, 279-304). Special thanks to *New York History* for permission to reprint this article.

1. See Heyer, "Patterns of Social Organizations in New York Chinatown," 54.

2. See Lau, "Traditionalism and Change in a Chinese American Community," 118.

3. See Stanford Lyman, "Conflict and the Web of Group Affiliation in San Francisco's Chinatown, 1850-1910," *The Asian in North America*, ed. Stanford Lyman (Santa Barbara, Calif.: American Bibliographical Center-Clio Press, 1977), 104.

4. K. Scott Wong, "Liang Qichao and the Chinese of America: A Re-evaluation of His Selected Memoir of Travels in the New World," *Journal of American Ethnic History*, Vol. 11, No. 4 (summer 1992), 10-11.

5. In his study of the San Francisco Chinese, Lyman did find the dichotomy between order and disunity in the Chinese community, but reasons for this dichotomy remain largely unexplored. See Lyman, "Conflict and the Web of Group Affiliation in San Francisco's Chinatown," 111-12.

6. Wu, *Hai Wai Yi Min Yu Hua Ren She Hui*, 292-93.

7. See Wong Chin Foo, "The Chinese in New York," 300; Jian-xiong Wu, *Hai Wai Yi Min Yu Hua Ren She Hui*, 293.

8. At first, immigrants from the same village in Guangdong and sharing the same surname formed a circle called a *Fang*. All the Fangs sharing the same surname were organized in turn into a family-name association.

9. Wu, *Hai Wai Yi Min Yu Hua Ren She Hui*, 292-96.

10. Leong Gor Yun, *Chinatown Inside Out* (New York: Barrows Mussey, 1936), 57.

11. Chu, *Eat a Bowl of Tea*, 148, 176.

12. Since in traditional Guangdong each village was usually inhabited by a whole lineage, fellow townsmen were often kinsmen as well. Thus, family-name associations and Hui Guans often overlapped each other both in terms of membership and leadership.

13. Consider, for example, the Lee Family Association, which was typical of the large Gong Suos in structure and functions. This association gave its members the privilege of borrowing money at a low interest rate and provided five-cent "free" meals for the aged and the unemployed. See Kuo, *Social and Political Change in New York's Chinatown*, 23.

14. *Lui Mei San Yi Zong Hui Guan Jian Shi (A Short History of the San Yi General Benevolent Association)*, 143.

15. *American Mosaic*, ed. Joan Morrison and Charlotte Fox Zabusky, 77.

16. Leung, "A Laundryman Sings the Blues," 14.

17. Chu, *Eat a Bowl of Tea*, 27.

18. Although occasionally we could find a few so-called family-name associations in traditional Guangdong, members of those organizations usually had a real blood loose line relationship. This was different from the largely fictive-kin nature of the Gong Suos among Chinese immigrants in the United States.

19. Alberto Pecorini, "The Italians in the United States," *Forum*, Vol. 45 (January 1911), 17, in *The Italians*, ed. Cordasco and Bucchioni, 155.

20. Alberto Pecorini, "The Italians in the United States," 17; Gino Speranza, "The Italians in Congested Districts," *Charities and Commons*, Vol. 20 (1908), 55, in *The Italians*, ed. Cordasco and Bucchioni, 140; and Jacob Riis, "Feast Days in Little Italy," *Century Magazine*, Vol. LVIII (August 1899), 494.

21. Leonard Covello, *The Heart Is the Teacher* (New York: McGraw Hill, 1958), 21-22.

22. *New York Times*, 8 March 1903.

23. Mangano, "The Associated Life of the Italians in New York City," *Charities*, Vol. 12 (1904), 482.

24. Gabaccia, *From Sicily to Elizabeth Street*, 103-4.

25. LaGumina, *The Immigrants Speak*, 54.

26. Virginia Yans-McLaughlin, *Family and Community: Italian Immigrants in Buffalo, 1880-1930* (Ithaca, N.Y.: Cornell University Press, 1977), 64-67.

27. Judith E. Smith, *Family Connections: A History of Italian and Jewish Immigrant Lives in Providence, Rhode Island, 1900-1940* (Albany, N.Y.: State University of New York Press, 1985), 104.

28. Odencrantz, *Italian Women in Industry*, 13-14.

29. Ware, *Greenwich Village*, 155-60.

30. Chinatown Study Group, *Chinatown Report 1969* (New York: n. p., 1970), 23, 38.

31. See "Reports on Conditions of Chinese Emigration by British Consuls to Their Home Government," *Hua Gong Chu Guo Shi Liao Hui Bian*, ed. Han-sheng Chen, Vol. 2, 9; Chan, *This Bittersweet Soil*, 386-87; Yung, *Unbound Feet*, 18-20.

32. For a detailed discussion of how institutional discrimination kept large numbers of Chinese women from immigrating to the United States, see Sucheng Chan, "The Exclusion of Chinese Women, 1870-1943," *Entry Denied*, ed. Sucheng Chan, especially 105-32; George A. Peffer, "Forbidden Families: Emigration Experiences of Chinese Women under the Page Law, 1875-1882," *Journal of American Ethnic History* (fall 1986), 28-46; see also Yung, *Unbound Feet*, 23-24.

33. Perhaps only in the Mafia did Italians organize themselves according to the family pattern. Values like subordination of an individual's interest to those of the group and submission to authority were often prerequisites for the harsh disciplines and concerted action of the Mafia, at least according to the largely anecdotal evidence available. Moreover, godparenting among Italian immigrants often facilitated the gathering of criminals, and the Mafia has often been referred to as a family business. Family feuds, a concomitant of close family ties, often motivated an individual to appeal for help to a mafiosi who would right his wrongs by extra-legal means. But the Mafia was not part of the regular social system and was limited only to a small number of people.

34. Chia-ling Kuo, for example, suggests that the more discriminatory the government policy of the host society was, the more united the Chinese community would become. See Kuo, *Social and Political Change in New York's Chinatown*, 18, 28.

35. Wong Chin Foo, "The Chinese in New York," 300.

36. *Lui Mei San Yi Zong Hui Guan Jian Shi*, 140.

37. Kuo, *Social and Political Change in New York's Chinatown*, 36, 38.

38. *Xin Bao*, 26 April 1946.

39. Chu, *East a Bowl of Tea*, 187, 197, 219, 223-24.

40. Mangano, "The Associated Life of the Italians in New York City," 479.

41. Mangano, "The Associated Life of the Italians in New York City," 479-80.

42. Broughton Brandenburg, *Imported Americans: The Story of the Experiences of a Disguised American and His Wife Studying the Immigration Question* (New York: F.A.

Stokes, 1904), 12. See also Charlotte Adams, "Italian Life in New York," *Harper's Magazine*, Vol. 62 (April 1881), in *The Italians*, ed. Cordasco and Bucchioni, 133.

43. In fact, the first constitution of the Order made it clear that the Order would work toward the "material and moral improvement of all American Italians." See Edwin Fenton, *Immigrants and Unions, a Case Study: Italians and American Labor, 1870-1920* (New York: Arno, 1975), 52, footnote.

44. Humbert Nelli, *Italians in Chicago, 1880-1930: A Study in Ethnic Mobility* (New York: Oxford University Press, 1975), 173-74.

45. Francesco Ragno, "Federation for Mutual-aid Associations," *United America*, 27 February 1926.

46. L. Eve Armentrout Ma, "Chinatown Organizations and the Anti-Chinese Movement, 1882-1914," in *Entry Denied*, ed. Chan, 159.

47. Ma, "Chinatown Organizations and the Anti-Chinese Movement," 153, 159.

48. *Min Qi Ri Bao*, 17 and 18 January 1928.

49. As a matter of fact, a Tseng Family Association was founded as late as in 1953 and a Hainan Hui Guan was established in 1956. See *Min Qi Ri Bao*, 14 August 1953, and 1 September 1956.

50. Over the years, a hierarchical system developed among the New York Chinese. Two super-regional associations, the Taishan-Ningyang Hui Guan and the Lian Cheng Association, ranked above all the surname and district organizations. The Taishan-Ningyang Hui Guan enlisted and claimed jurisdiction over all the family and district organizations that originated in the Taishan area in Guangdong. The Lian Cheng Association represented all other regional and family-name associations. The two super-regional associations were subordinate to the Chinese Consolidated Benevolent Association, which arose out of the necessity of coordinating relations between the various associations.

51. "Notice of the CCBA," *Guo Quan Bao*, 13 January 1923; *Mei Zhou Hua Qiao Ri Bao*, 29 and 30 January 1948. See also Leong, *Chinatown Inside Out*, 36, 38.

52. Beck, *New York's Chinatown*, 18.

53. See *Min Qi Ri Bao*, 7, 8, and 20 September 1938, and *Xin Bao*, 23 November 1943.

54. *Min Qi Ri Bao*, 23 July 1954.

55. *Min Qi Ri Bao*, 1 April 1950, and 3 April 1957. See also *Saturday Evening Post*, 18 March 1951, 18, 39.

56. *Mei Zhou Hua Qiao Ri Bao*, 7 August 1941. The justification for forming this association is that the four family names—Tan, Tan, Xu, and Xie—share a common radical (the two Tans represent two different Chinese characters). It was assumed that the ancestors of the New York Chinese sharing these surnames must be related.

57. See *Xin Bao*, 26 April 1946.

58. In the late nineteenth century, disappointed at China's backwardness and weakness, a group of intellectuals headed by Kang You-wei convinced Emperor Guangxu of the necessity of reform. Through reforming the government and introducing Western technology into China, these reformers hoped, China would be able to catch up with Western powers. But, outnumbered by diehards, the reform was soon defeated.

59. Ma, "Chinatown Organizations and the Anti-Chinese Movement," 156-59.

60. For information on the Chinese reformers' activities in New York City, see *New York Times*, 28 June 1905. Pei Chi Liu, *Mei Guo Hua Qiao Shi (History of the Chinese in the United States)*, 447. See also K. Scott Wong, "Liang Qichao and the Chinese of America," 7, 10.

61. Kuo, *Social and Political Change in New York's Chinatown*, 38.

62. According to a contemporary New York Chinese, it would take $100 to open a laundry in New York City in the late nineteenth century, obviously unaffordable for an individual Chinese. See Wong Chin Foo, "The Chinese in New York," 298.

63. Leung, "A Laundryman Sings the Blues," 14; Beck, *New York's Chinatown*, 61; Yu, *To Save China, To Save Ourselves*, 11.

64. Wong Chin Foo, "The Chinese in New York," 25; S. T. Chen, "A Review of the Past Ten Years and a Look into the Future," *Mei Zhou Hua Qiao Ri Bao*, 26 April 1943. Chen was then a leading member of the Chinese Hand Laundry Alliance of New York.

65. *Min Qi Ri Bao*, 7 August 1941; Beck, *New York's Chinatown*, 61; and Glick, *Shake Hands with the Dragon*, 166, 172.

66. According to a *Harper's Weekly* report of 1888, many New York Chinese lived with their kinsmen in the boarding houses. See *Harper's Weekly*, 1 December 1888, 918. For more examples see *Eat a Bowl of Tea*, 35. In 1918, the residents at 13, 16, 19, and 36 Mott Street and 31 and 34 Pell Street were all of a Taishan origin, while those who took up abode at 4 Mott Street and 4 Doyers Street hailed from Heshan and Xinhui respectively. See *Who's Who of the Chinese in New York*, 25-85.

67. Chu, *Eat a Bowl of Tea*, 35.

68. See Glick, *Shake Hands with the Dragon*, 166.

69. *Eat a Bowl of Tea*, 71-72, 138. For more discussion of the underdevelopment of class consciousness among the New York Chinese, see chapter 6.

70. *New York Times*, 27 February 1955. "To his customers and other acquaintances, he [Chinese laundryman] is a thing and a stereotype," observed sociologist Paul Siu in the early 1950s. "Only to his fellow Chinese is he a person. . . . Wherever he may have been, he does not forget to pay a visit to Chinatown where he feels more at home, where he shops for daily necessities . . . and, above all, where he is recognized as a person." See Paul Siu, *The Chinese Laundrymen*, 137, 145. See also Sing Jang Leung's autobiography, "A Laundryman Sings the Blues," 20.

71. See Glick, *Shake Hands with the Dragon*, 191; see also Chu, *Eat a Bowl of Tea*, 28.

72. See *Mei Zhou Hua Qiao Ri Bao*, 4 March 1958. According to Robert Lamb Hart's study, there were 125 garment factories in New York's Chinatown in the mid-1960s employing 6,000 to 8,000 workers. This means that each clothing factory hired on average forty to sixty people. Needless to say, some bigger factories could hire more than one hundred people. See Robert Lamb Hart, Adam Krivatsy, and William Stubee, *New York Chinatown: A Report on the Conditions and Needs of a Unique Community* (New York: n. p., 1968), 27.

73. Kwong, *The New Chinatown*, 144.

74. Kwong, *The New Chinatown*, 64, 152. For more information on New York Chinatown strikes after the 1960s, see chapter 6.

75. Elizabeth J. Perry, *Shanghai on Strike: The Politics of Chinese Labor* (Stanford, Calif.: Stanford University Press, 1993), 29.

76. This newly emerged community unity, of course, was not limited to strikes. In 1975, more than 2,500 New York Chinatown residents took part in a demonstration to protest the beating of a Chinese American by the fifth precinct police. Mak Nui, an eighty-year-old participant, said to a *New York Times* reporter, "I am going to join the demonstration because I am Chinese." While she said this, her eighty-one-year-old friend, Tsuen Po Tzi, expressed her approval. See *New York Times*, 13 May 1975.

77. Kwong, *The New Chinatown*, 143-46.

78. Kwong, *The New Chinatown*, 151-52.

79. Kuo, *Social and Political Change in New York's Chinatown*, 10-11, 45.

80. Elizabeth Bogen, *Immigration in New York* (New York: Praeger, 1987), 106.

81. See, for example, David M. Gordon, Richard Edwards, and Michael Reich, *Segmented Work, Divided Workers: The Historical Transformation of Labor in the United States* (Cambridge, England: Cambridge University Press, 1982), especially 73-78, 165-227.

82. *Mei Zhou Hua Qiao Ri Bao*, 18 February 1952, and 12 April 1958.

83. See Dean Lan, "Chinatown Sweatshops," in *Counterpoints: Perspectives on Asian-America*, 351-52; and *Mei Zhou Hua Qiao Ri Bao*, 14 April 1958.

6

Labor Militancy

For a long time, Chinese immigrant workers were viewed by organized labor and some scholars as docile and incapable of expressing labor militancy.[1] This allegation has now been laid to rest by many recent studies, which have shown that Chinese immigrants demonstrated labor militancy in California as early as the 1860s.[2] But there is no denying the fact that those early strikes were transient and did not lead to the formation of viable trade unions. With few exceptions, the overwhelming majority of Chinese immigrants remained non-unionized until the 1960s.

Scholars have seldom systematically explored the reasons for the lack of labor militancy among Chinese immigrants. One may very well assume that aloofness of Chinese immigrants from trade unionism was due to labor's hostility toward them. Such an interpretation, however, cannot explain why many Chinese were reluctant to join the union when some labor organizations approached them and urged them to do so. Through studying the effects of occupational discrimination against Chinese immigrants, this chapter demonstrates that by confining the Chinese to self-employed and quasi-family firms, racism reduced the chance for Chinese immigrant workers to become class conscious. It also explores the leading role of Chinese artisans in expressing labor militancy and demonstrates that racial discrimination reduced the number of Chinese artisans in New York and therefore deprived Chinese immigrant workers of effective leadership.

Here, again, the Italian experience serves as an excellent point of reference, because in the beginning both groups were widely regarded as strikebreakers by the established labor movement. But by the 1910s, many Italians became identified with the American labor movement and began striking against their employers while the Chinese did not take similar action until half a century later. Studying the reasons that led Italians to reverse their previous aloofness from trade unionism will help us better understand the relationship between Chinese immigrants and the American labor movement.

I

A brief look at the situation in the early 1890s suggests that indifference to trade unionism characterized both immigrant groups in New York. Southern Italian peasants did not arrive in New York as labor activists. In fact, a number of factors in Italian tradition worked against their involvement in the labor movement. Dreaming of becoming small landholders in their native villages, southern Italian immigrants were not easily convinced to unionize and to fight for the improvement of their plight.[3] For several decades, regional loyalties carried over from Italy kept the New York Italian community divided.[4] This situation certainly was not conducive to the working-class unity among Italian immigrants. Most of the job contractors *(padroni)* always did their best to discourage the *contadini* from becoming class conscious. At the same time, Italian tradition also discouraged young women from leaving their homes at night without chaperons. As a result, many Italian female workers could not attend the meetings organized by labor unions.[5]

But Italians' aloofness from unionism began to shift to a kind of activism shortly after the turn of the century, when Italian laborers working for the subways walked off the job, demanding higher wages and shorter hours. Under the leadership of Salvatore Ninfo, a socialist, they organized themselves into a labor union. These construction workers were soon followed by Italian dressmakers who joined the striking New York dressmakers in 1909.[6] By the early 1910s, union drives had appeared among Italian cloak and shirt makers, men's dressmakers, ladies' tailors and dressmakers, painters and papers hangers in New York City.[7] This headway, however, was not achieved without setbacks and relapses. In fact, spontaneity and transiency were characteristics of those early strikes. Most strikes staged by Italian construction workers, for example, were not well planned; many of them were spontaneous walkouts. When conditions became unbearable, the men would put forward their demands for better treatment and, if refused, lay down their tools. Moreover, when the strikes were over, especially when their demands were met, unions would be disbanded.[8] During the first decade of the twentieth century, most Italian workers in New York remained unorganized.

The 1910s marked a turning point in Italian American labor history. This was the decade in which Italian immigrants began to forsake their sojourner mentality, and many labor militants joined their fellow countrymen in the New World. But efforts to bring Italian immigrant workers into the established unions were under way even before the 1910s. Italian plasterers' helpers, mosaic workers' helpers, and hod carriers in New York became unionized as early as the 1890s. In 1903, under the auspices of Tito Pacelli, an official from the Mason's Union, and Herman Robinson, a representative of the American Federation of Labor, the Rockmen's and Excavators' Union was founded. Hundreds of Italians became members of the union, and thousands more became its sympathizers.[9] Italians, in sum, were most likely to become unionized where their work was closely related to that of the skilled workers and when the skilled workers' support was available. The New York garment workers' walkout in 1912 witnessed almost ten thousand Italian home finishers join the strikers. When the strike was over, Italian garment workers had not only become unionized, but also stayed in the unions as loyal members.[10] In 1919, there was established on East 14th Street an Italian Chamber of Labor, whose purpose was "spreading the principles and ethics of labor unionism and helping all recognized labor unions in their industrial and educational activities among the Italian speaking workers."[11] The succeeding decade saw labor unions spread into Italian artificial flowers and spaghetti workers, piano makers, furniture workers, and pastry and ice cream workers.[12] In the mid-1930s, approximately 100,000 out of a total membership of 250,000 of the International Ladies Garment Workers' Union for Greater New York were either Italian immigrants or their children. At the same time, there were 100,000 Italians organized in various branches of the building trades' unions and many thousands organized in the Amalgamated Clothing Worker's Union.[13]

Unlike the Italians, the majority of Chinese immigrants in New York for many decades did not stage strikes against their employers, nor were they identified with the American labor movement. In 1919, the Industrial Workers of the World managed to enlist several dozen young Chinese restaurant workers in New York, who demanded a pay increase from their employers. But before these unionists could achieve anything, Chinatown's elite declared war on them and, under pressure from the whole community, most of the unionists withdrew.[14] Aloofness from trade unionism and radicalism continued to characterize the New York Chinese in the next four decades. In 1928, a *New York Times* reporter witnessed the indifference of Chinatown's residents to the propaganda of the radicals:

> Under a scorching sun, a crowd of over 500, made up mostly of Chinese, yesterday afternoon stood for two hours on the corner of Mott and Pell Streets listening to speakers of the All-American Anti-Imperialistic League explain their ideas of the politics of Wall Street, Japan and Great Britain. The speeches were made both in English and Chinese and though little enthusiasm was forthcoming from the onlookers, except when Japan was denounced, the crowd remained to the end.[15]

In the 1930s, the leftists in New York's Chinatown[16] tried to arouse class consciousness among the Chinese immigrant workers and organize them along class lines. These leftists were hoping that, through their repeated propaganda, workers would view their employers as enemies. However, the leftists' endeavor met with very limited success. On July 1, 1933, for example, they initiated a contest, hoping to have one hundred copies of their semi monthly newspaper *Xian Feng Bao (The Chinese Vanguard)* sold to the Chinese workers in New

York. By August, however, only twenty-eight copies had been sold. [17] The reasons for this failure, observed the editor in an earlier editorial, "was the lack of efforts on the part of our comrades and lack of a deep understanding of the significance of the *Vanguard* on the part of the readers."[18]

In the early 1950s, the Committee for Industrial Organization (CIO) initiated a campaign aimed at recruiting the Chinese laundrymen in New York into the union. When they found the Chinese stubborn, the unionists decided to picket those laundries. This move caused a great deal of panic among the Chinese, who urgently mobilized to resist the CIO's membership drive.[19] *Mei Zhou Hua Qiao Ri Bao*, a newspaper backed by the Chinese Hand Laundry Alliance of New York, pointed out that Chinese laundries were all small businesses whose nature was different from big American companies. The paper went on to beseech the CIO to stop its membership drive among the Chinese.[20] Strikes against their employers did eventually take place among Chinese immigrant workers in New York, but those happened only toward the end of the 1950s when the Chinese laundrymen struck against a cut in wages[21] and when the women garment workers struck for higher pay.[22] After the 1960s, increasing numbers of Chinese in New York also became members of established labor organizations such as the International Ladies Garment Workers' Union.

II

Why were the Italians able to reverse their previous aloofness from unionism and join organized labor during the 1910s while the Chinese could not do so until half a century later? Any attempt to explain this huge difference between the two immigrant groups in labor activism must begin with a discussion of the discrimination against the Chinese by the established labor unions. In California, it was the Workingmen's Party that spearheaded the anti-Chinese movement. The two major labor unions—the Knights of Labor and the American Federation of Labor—were not only behind the agitations for Chinese exclusion but also refused to accept Chinese laborers as union members.[23] President Samuel Gompers of the AFL made it clear time and again that his union would never give membership to Chinese immigrants even though they were skilled workers. The hostility of organized labor was to a great extent responsible for the failure of Chinese immigrants to be associated with the labor movement. Although in the beginning labor unions in New York such as the bricklayers also rejected the Italians for their strikebreaking activities, this negative attitude did not last long. After 1900, the American Federation of Labor began to take steps to recruit Italian immigrants.[24] In terms of being accepted by organized labor, Italians definitely enjoyed an advantage over their Chinese counterparts.

But it would be simplistic to jump to the conclusion that labor's hostility toward the Chinese was the only factor shaping those immigrants' aloofness from unionism. After all, the Wobblies had tried to recruit Chinese and other Asian immigrants in the early twentieth century. Most New York Chinese, however, did not express much interest in this industrial union. Instead, they forced those few who joined to withdraw.[25] Although on the national level the Knights of Labor was anti-Chinese, some of the Knights' local offices expressed a different attitude due to the autonomy those locals enjoyed. For example, a New York City local assembly of the Knights (No. 49) twice made the effort to recruit the Chinese. Under its socialist leadership, this assembly organized two groups of Chinese in the mid-1880s.[26] But its effort to secure charters for the Chinese was frustrated by the strong opposition from the General Executive Board of the Knights.[27] In 1893, Local 49 demanded the repeal of the Chinese Exclusion Act on the ground that "these laborers have built railways and reclaimed swamp lands and irrigated deserts, and thus increased the supply and diminished the cost of food."[28] Two years later, probably encouraged by such a statement, some Chinese laundrymen in New York attempted to organize a union that was to be affiliated with District Assembly 49.[29] Unfortunately, the pressure from Terence Powderly, the former Grand Master Workman, compelled those Chinese who joined the Knights to leave. But on both occasions not many Chinese were attracted to the union, either.

These episodes and the CIO's unsuccessful membership drive suggest that in addition to labor's hostility, something else was at work that discouraged Chinese workers from showing interest in trade unionism—the immigrant workers' reluctance to fight their employers. In fact, Italian immigrants became identified with the labor movement not only as a result of labor's willingness to accept them but also because of their willingness to battle their employers for better treatment. But why did Italians express labor militancy so much earlier than the Chinese? To answer this question, we must study the economic adjustment of the two immigrant groups.

As mentioned in chapter 3, in the late nineteenth and early twentieth centuries, most New York Italians found employment in the manufacturing and construction trades. The number of Italians entering skilled occupations was also fairly large.[30] Chinese immigrants, however, could not but engage in such small businesses as laundries, restaurants, and grocery stores, and a considerable number of them were self-employed. The result of such major differences in occupations for Italian and Chinese immigrants was quite significant. Their earlier integration into the U.S. economic structure provided Italian immigrants with an opportunity to intermingle with the mainstream labor force. According to *Harper's Magazine*, as early as 1881 Italian workmen in New York were already "found everywhere mingled with those of other nationalities."[31] At the turn of the century, Italian masons constituted 18 percent of the masons in New York City. In 1910, 10,000 to 20,000 out of a total of 50,000 cloak, suit, and skirt makers in New York were Italian. In 1912, Italians were at least one third of the longshoremen of that city.[32]

Moreover, because most contadini became unskilled laborers in New York, they were faced directly with exploitative employers. The experience of Italian longshoremen in Brooklyn presented a good example of this kind of confrontation. Each morning, Italians, together with dock workers of other nationalities, had to wait at the pier heads for hours to see if they could be hired. The highly competitive nature of the job market and the tendency of hiring the men by the hour often enabled the foremen to receive bribery through "kick-back," a considerable portion of one day's pay.[33] Experiences like this undoubtedly nurtured hatred toward their employers. "Until they were employed and organized into a crew," observed a labor historian, "there was no institution around which they could rally and no clearly perceptible enemy. But once on a construction job, a crew became informally organized and had a focus for its resentment."[34] On August 20, 1891, for example, a group of twenty-five *braccianti* (laborers) in Brooklyn pursued Charles Kinderman, a labor contractor. These laborers beat the contractor with sticks and attacked him with stones. All this was because the contractor failed to pay the laborers on time.[35] Among Italian immigrants, therefore, there developed a potential for labor militancy: In due time, they would be convinced by the radicalism preached by labor leaders and socialists.

The Italian experiences in other cities also suggest the importance of economic opportunity for labor militancy. A good example was presented by Tampa, Florida, a city well-known for its labor unrest in the early twentieth century. The general strikes of 1901, 1910, and 1920 by Tampa's cigarmakers all witnessed the active participation of Italian immigrants. During the 1910 walkout, Italians were not only the mainstay of the protest but also the most reluctant to return to work when the strike was defeated. Evidently, the concentration of Italians in an industry (by 1910, close to 20 percent of the city's cigarmakers were Italian) dominated by exploitative Spanish employers fostered these immigrant workers' labor militancy. In contrast, in New Orleans where most Italians were engaged in small-scale trades and commerce, and in San Francisco where Italians often worked as fishermen, labor militancy never fully developed among these southern European immigrants.[36] Indeed, the situation of Italians in New Orleans and San Francisco was somewhat similar to that of the New York Chinese.

The concentration of Chinese immigrants in small businesses generated results unfavorable for labor militancy. Since many of the New York Chinese working in restaurants and laundries were self-employed, there was little chance for them to be mingled with the city's labor force. Strictly speaking, because they were self-employed, these people were not part of the working class no matter how menial their jobs were and how hard-working they could be. Because class consciousness is generated from the confrontation between the employer and the employee, we cannot expect these self-employed Chinese to become class conscious.

As mentioned in the previous chapter, some firms did need employees. But, segregated from the larger society's economy, these firms mostly hired Chinese workers, especially kinsmen and fellow townsmen. Often, employees of the restaurants and laundries were partners as well.[37] Almost as a rule, the owners worked together with their employees, because the work in such firms was labor intensive and the division of labor was not clear. Because most employees in the restaurants and laundries were either kin from the same lineage or fellow townsmen, a kind of family atmosphere always permeated the workplace: People addressed each other in kinship terms that served to minimize possible antagonistic feelings between the employer and the employee. Confined to the family or quasi-family firms, these Chinese employees had no more chance to become class conscious than their self-employed brethren. Though in the 1930s the Chinese Hand Laundry Alliance, a newly emerged organization with some democratic principles, challenged Chinatown's merchant elite in many ways, the CHLA was, in the last analysis, a trade guild rather than a labor union. Lian-ai Tan, a leading figure of the CHLA in the 1940s, testified to the absence of class consciousness in an article entitled "Chinese Laundrymen and Trade Unionism." Tan stated in 1941:

> In order to organize unions, we must first of all find out whether or not the people to be organized are inclined to unionism. Consider, for example, Chinese laundries. Among the Chinese laundrymen there is not a clear line of demarcation between the employer and the worker. Often, the laundry owners are themselves workers. Many of them do not hire workers; when they do, they employ their cousins or friends. As for treatment, we all know that the hired men eat, work and even live together with their employers. Because of the non-existence of a line between capital and labor, there is no necessity to organize unions. . . . The central task of the CHLA is not to find a way to increase wages and to sign contracts with employers, but to help the members take care of the affairs of their laundries.[38]

Here, the precise kind of employment relationship Chinese immigrant workers entered into in the United States was the determining factor. It seems that when they worked for white employers, away from the Chinese familial and district network, a certain degree of distrust for their employers might develop. In 1867, Chinese workers thus staged a large-scale strike against the Central Pacific Railroad Company, exhibiting tremendous militancy. Six years later, Chinese crewmen working for the Pacific Mail line successfully conducted another strike.[39] In 1884, Chinese cigar workers employed by white proprietors in San Francisco walked out, demanding higher wages. In the fall of the same year, they struck again, this time asking for "closed shop."[40] Some Chinese workers were also seen attending the meetings organized by the United Mine Workers of America in Rock Springs, Wyoming, in 1908.[41] But it was still questionable whether the militancy manifested in those strikes was really class consciousness, because the Chinese involved in those early strikes probably organized themselves vertically "into an all-Chinese guild," rather than horizontally as wage-earners against their employers.[42] Nevertheless, given time, the distrust might have developed into class consciousness.

When immigrants expressed militancy, the attitude of organized labor became crucial: Its willingness to accept the immigrants would facilitate the latter's integration into the established labor movement. In the middle of a strike by Italian construction workers in 1903, for example, the AFL issued charters to the newly founded Rockmen's and Excavators' Union, which helped the Italians win some strikes in the following years.[43] But when the Chinese struck in 1885, white unions not only failed to extend any help but also accused the Chinese of "feeling overbearing in their strength."[44] On those occasions, the Chinese struck on their own initiative.

In contrast, when the immigrants worked for Chinese employers, especially when they entered the Chinese familial and district network, as in the case of restaurants and laundries in New York City, a kind of employer-employee collaboration most likely prevailed. Under such circumstances, even if organized labor groups had approached the Chinese, these Asian immigrants would probably still have been unwilling to join American workers in bargaining with their Chinese employers. This perhaps explains why in the early 1950s when the CIO approached the Chinese laundrymen in New York, the latter tried to ward off the union drive instead of welcoming it as a good opportunity to join the labor movement. An interesting case was offered earlier by the Chinese cigarmakers. According to a *New York Tribune* report of 1885, two hundred out of a total of three hundred Chinese cigarmakers in New York had organized themselves "into an efficient trade union, which meets weekly at No. 30 Pell Street." The *Tribune* did not explain why these Chinese became unionized, but it did indicate that most of these cigarmakers were employed by the Cuban cigar manufacturers in Maiden Lane.[45] This example reinforces the argument that, faced with non-Chinese employers, Chinese workers were more inclined toward labor militancy.

The case of a group of Chinese laundrymen working in New Jersey presents an even better example showing that employment relationships were the key to labor militancy. In the early 1870s, James B. Harvey, the owner of a steam laundry in Belleville, New Jersey, brought 160 Chinese from San Francisco to replace the Irish women who often went on strikes. We do not know how many workers Harvey employed altogether, but it is said that after his successor expanded the business in the 1880s, the laundry hired 275 people, including 75 Chinese. It can be reasonably assumed, therefore, that Harvey probably hired about 200 workers in the 1870s. Under such circumstances, the 160 Chinese definitely made up the great majority of his work force.

And in this case the Asians proved to be no less militant than their Irish counterparts. According to the Newark (New Jersey) *Sunday Call*, as soon as the Chinese "learned how white employees gained financial advantage by striking, there was a series of walkouts and labor disputes."[46] "The Chinese even went so far as to strike," observed *North Jersey Highlander*. "They were beginning to become more and more like their white neighbors." They were also said to have chased their employers with knives.[47] The Chinese continued their striking activities until they were fired by Harvey's successor in 1885. Many of these Chinese laundrymen later on moved to New York City to work.[48] But they staged no strikes there in the subsequent years. In New York, they either became self-employed or worked for Chinese employers. The Chinese were militant in nearby New Jersey but became inactive in New York. This difference was undoubtedly the result of changed employment relations.

The San Francisco Chinese garment workers' strike in the late 1930s might be the only exception to this general pattern: It was a walkout against Chinese employers and, at the same time, received financial as well as moral support from white-led unions. In the middle of the Great Depression, the International Ladies Garment Workers' Union lifted its ban on Chinese members and sent several representatives to San Francisco's Chinatown to organize the garment workers there.[49] Meanwhile, trouble was brewing in Chinatown's sweatshops due to the employers' refusal to raise wages for their workers. Finally, in 1938, the seamstresses working for Chinatown's largest garment factory, the National Dollar Stores, walked out and organized themselves into Local 341 of the ILGWU. "So far as anybody knows," observed *Time*, these "were the first Chinese picket lines in the U.S."[50] Owing partly to the support from the established unions such as the ILGWU and the AFL, the strike was briefly victorious.[51]

But, while the strike did seem to be an exception, if we take a close look at the motives behind the strike and the employment structure of San Francisco Chinatown's garment factories, this episode did not totally contradict our earlier argument about the importance of employment relationship for labor militancy. First, behind the seamstresses' demand for higher wages, there was a strong desire to send money to China to support their families and to contribute to the war against the Japanese invasion.[52] Second, perhaps more importantly, the structure of the San Francisco Chinese garment factories was different from that of New York's Chinese laundries. The National Dollar Stores, for example, hired almost two hundred people in the 1930s. The relatively large size of the workplace probably made it difficult for the kinship and district networks to function in harmonizing the employer-worker relationship. This state of affairs, in fact, heralded a similar situation in New York's Chinatown two decades later.

The fact that the New York Chinese community began to witness more and more labor disputes after the 1950s further substantiates the importance of the employment relationship in accounting for Chinese labor militancy. By the late 1960s, almost all Chinatown seamstresses had joined the International Ladies

Garment Workers' Union.[53] In the previous chapter, we mentioned an unprecedented, large-scale strike by the Chinese garment workers in 1982 when their employers failed to agree on a wage increase. Almost 20,000 workers walked out, eventually forcing their Chinese employers to compromise.[54] After the mid-1960s, class consciousness also began to develop among Chinese laundry and restaurant workers in New York. In 1971, for example, the Chinese ironing workers began to organize themselves and demanded that the management increase their wages.[55]

The Chinese restaurant workers, though they lagged behind the seamstresses in being unionized, also became militant after the 1960s. Strikes and union activities first began with the restaurants outside Chinatown, but eventually spread into Chinatown proper. In 1980, Chinatown's biggest and most elegant restaurant, Silver Palace, fired fifteen waiters after a dispute, which touched off militant actions on the part of the workers. A picket line was formed and donations from workers in other restaurants helped build up the morale. The victory, in the end, was the workers'.[56]

Playing no small part in bringing about these dramatic changes since the 1950s was the transformation of the economic structure of the New York Chinese community. As mentioned earlier, the Chinese garment industry rose to importance in the 1960s, which represented the beginning of an enclave economy. Since these factories usually hired dozens, sometimes even hundreds, of people, they were characterized by a clear-cut division between labor and management. Moreover, because of their relatively large size, the garment factories could no longer hire solely kinsmen or fellow townspeople. In fact, many of the garment workers had few connections with the established familial and district ties in Chinatown because they were mostly new immigrants from Hong Kong and from other parts of China. Consequently, the garment workers were confronted directly with the often exploitative Chinese employers. To some extent, this situation was also true of the laundry and restaurant workers. Such circumstances were unquestionably conducive to the development of class consciousness among the Chinese immigrant workers.

The urban background of the new immigrants should also be taken into account in understanding the labor militancy that emerged in Chinatown in the 1960s. As a typical capitalist society in the Far East, Hong Kong familiarized its residents with the experiences in the wage-labor system and with a modern concept of patron-client relationship. Unlike the old timers from the rural areas in Guangdong, therefore, the new immigrants who grew up in Hong Kong were less familiar with traditional Chinese values such as familism and lineage solidarity. For the immigrants from Hong Kong, labor unions and collective bargaining were nothing new. A *Mei Zhou Hua Qiao Qi Bao* report of 1965 tells us that in Hong Kong almost every trade had a labor union and even the house maids were unionized.[57]

We must also remember that after the Communists took over China in

1949, "class struggle" not only became a frequently used term, but was also put into practice in the country's political life: Peasants were taught to fight their landlords and workers their employers. Much more than their predecessors from Guangdong, therefore, those who migrated from mainland China after the 1940s were familiar with the notion of class struggle. Not surprisingly, these new immigrants stood up for their rights when conditions became intolerable.

III

Earlier we pointed out that integration into the larger society's economy enabled Italian immigrants to develop labor militancy. But economic opportunities were not the sole reason for the Italians' earlier involvement in the labor movement. In fact, the Italians' earlier participation in trade unions was due in no small part to the leadership provided by Italian artisans and socialists. In 1916, tailors, shoemakers, carpenters, and other skilled craftsmen made up more than 15 percent of the total Italian labor force in New York City.[58] New York was an artisan crowded city—to use Donna Gabaccia's term—, where most Italian artisans did not have much chance to become immigrant *prominenti* (elite) but stayed in their old occupations.[59] The continuation of the old trades made it possible for these artisans to stick to their Old World radicalism.

Italian barbers in New York were perhaps the first to organize and to strike. Though Italian journeymen barbers often thought their interests were aligned with those of their employers, they threatened to strike in New York in May 1886, together with barbers of other nationalities, demanding a thirteen-hour day. In the end the employers gave in and met the journeymen's demand.[60] Italian masons in New York demonstrated their eagerness to unionize as early as 1890.[61] In 1891, a Stone Masons Union located on Broome Street decided to join the Knights of Labor.[62]

Italian artisans' labor activism was inseparable from the influence of Italian socialists. What Italian socialists did at first, as table 6.1 indicates, was to organize the artisans into mutual-aid societies. Some of these mutual-aid societies eventually became labor unions. In addition, Italian socialists provided leadership for the garment workers, barbers, and workers in the building trade. They also managed to build a bridge between Italian immigrant workers and the major labor organizations such as the Knights of Labor. Nicola Conforti, for example, was at once both a mason and a well-known Italian socialist in New York City.[63]

Italian artisans' radicalism was mainly an Old World product. In Italy, especially northern Italy, artisans and factory workers were often believers in class struggle and group action. The formation of mutual-aid societies in the late nineteenth century represented the early stage of the artisans' group action.[64]

Table 6.1. Mutual-Aid Societies Founded by Socialists in New York City, 1882-1896

Year	Societies
1882	Pastry Cooks
1885	Barbers
1886	Garment Workers
1886	Masons
1886	Shoe Workers
1891	Musicians
1896	Woodworkers

Source: Edwin Fenton, *Immigrants and Unions, a Case Study: Italians and American Labor, 1870-1920* (New York: Arno, 1975), 160.

More importantly, by the time large-scale overseas emigration was underway, many mutual-aid societies were already functioning as trade unions. Strikes, for example, were often organized by these mutual-aid societies. Meanwhile, parliamentary socialists also began to enlist supporters in Italy. By 1892, socialists of various tones, except anarchists, were able to rally under the banner of the Italian Socialist Party, although the party soon ran into trouble because of internal strife. But the radicalism preached by the socialists did not disappear with the emergence of the strife. In fact, quite a few socialists migrated to the United States and became leaders of the artisan groups in the eastern cities.[65] Nicola Gigliotti, the most important union leader among Italian bricklayers in New York, had been a trade union organizer for bricklayers near Pozzouli, Italy, in the late 1880s and had been a socialist candidate during elections.[66]

But to emphasize Italian artisans' labor activism does not imply that class consciousness was only limited to the skilled craftsmen. As a matter of fact, before large-scale emigration was underway, a kind of class consciousness had also developed among the contadini in many parts of southern Italy. In the late nineteenth and early twentieth centuries, as a result of the vestiges of feudalism, class distinctions in southern Italy were quite discernible, with the contadini occupying the bottom of the social ladder. Since the meager income from tilling their own small parcels of land was not sufficient for supporting their families, the contadini often had to work for the large landowners in order to supplement their income. Exploitation was common.[67] The contadini, exploited and downtrodden, harbored bitter hatred toward the *signori* (gentry).[68] "*Sfruttamento* (exploitation)," observed a student of Italian immigration, "was the expression of the southern *contadini* when they compared themselves with anyone who did not belong to their class."[69]

Before the mid-1850s, the Italian peasant movement in southern Italy was often marked by violence. But by the late nineteenth century, many peasants had learned to right their wrongs by quasi-political means. In 1848, a peasant revolt in Sambuca, Sicily, witnessed the burning of the local population registers and the assault on the tax collector. But that was the last jacquerie-type revolt in Sambuca. After this episode, the peasants began to adopt new forms of protest such as staging agricultural strikes and voting for the socialist candidates.[70] This new form of agricultural protest, in fact, was typical of many other parts of Sicily. Most likely related to the rise of rural capitalism, a widespread peasant movement in Sicily in the late nineteenth century called the *Fasci* contained many new elements that gave this movement a modern political tinge, though it still found "expression in traditional millenarian terms."[71] Riots continued, but more often the movement took a political form, for example, the founding of peasant leagues under socialist leadership and the staging of agricultural strikes.[72] Its goals included a wide variety of demands like the increase of wages, division of land, municipal reform, and abolition of taxes and excise.[73] As table 6.2 indicates, during the late nineteenth and early twentieth centuries, agricultural strikes were a widespread phenomenon in the rural areas of Italy. Despite the gap between northern and southern Italy in terms of the number of strikes and participants in the strikes, the fact that labor activism was on the rise in south Italy and Sicily is unequivocal.

Our earlier discussion of the role of Italian artisans naturally raises the question: Did Chinese artisans and skilled workers in New York also lead the peasant immigrants in demonstrating labor militancy? Here, the lack of sources prevents us from making a sweeping conclusion. But sporadic sources do suggest that the different attitudes of the Chinese toward matters such as labor unionism probably also had something to do with the occupational backgrounds of these immigrants. In 1884, for example, some fifty naturalized Chinese in New York's Chinatown held a conference and organized themselves into a political association. The secretary of the conference condemned the Republican Party for passing the anti-Chinese bill[74] and referred to the Democrats as robbers and thieves. Li Quong, who was made temporary chairman of the meeting, was president of the Chinese Cigarmakers' Union.[75]

In the 1880s, there were two dozen skilled workers among the New York Chinese in addition to the cigarmakers.[76] This number had decreased by 1918, at which time there were only three carpenters, two electricians, six machinists, and six tailors in the New York Chinese community.[77] But it is interesting to note the situation of Chinese cigarmakers in New York. As mentioned earlier, many Chinese cigarmakers were unionized in the mid-1880s. The 1885 *New York Tribune* report counted three hundred cigarmakers in New York's China-town,[78] but three decades later, Chinese cigarmakers had almost disappeared from the city.[79] Because in the nineteenth century cigarmakers were highly skilled, perhaps we can reasonably assume that, before the mid-1880s when the Chinese Exclusion Act went into effect, the number of Chinese artisans and skilled workers in New York was relatively high. Probably for that reason, Chinatown exhibited a certain degree of labor militancy and political activism during that time.

Table 6.2. Agricultural Labor Unions (1907) and Strikes (1901-1904) among Agricultural Laborers in Italy

Location	Unions	Membership	Strikes	Participants
North Italy	289	49,884	701	171,911
South Italy & Sicily	248	92,227	65	70,923
Total	537	142,111	766	242,834

Source: Reports of the Immigration Commission, Vol. 4, 161, Table 17 (condensed).

But after the 1880s, with the vigorous enforcement of the Chinese Exclusion Act, the number of Chinese artisans as well as peasant immigrants became much smaller. While Chinese artisans and peasant immigrants were both victims of racial discrimination, there is reason to believe that the artisans were particularly hard hit. New York always attracted many artisans due to the many opportunities the city offered. Not surprisingly, native-born artisans were jealous of their foreign, especially non-white, rivals. The strong anti-foreign sentiments might be responsible for the passage of a series of New York State laws restricting alien artisans' employment opportunities.[80] As a result, the number of Chinese skilled workmen in New York City sharply decreased by the early twentieth century. As the number of Chinese artisans declined, so did labor militancy and political activism in the Chinese community. If the argument on the role played by artisans is valid, then the number of artisans who came to New York, together with the number of peasant immigrants, was an important factor underlaying the immigrants' labor activism. It should be noted that, in comparison with other European immigrants such as the Jews, Italian artisans were rather small in number. As a result, they often lagged behind the Jews and some other European immigrants in terms of unionization.[81] But when compared with that of the Chinese, the proportion of Italian artisans was substantially higher. The lack of a sizeable artisan group most likely deprived the New York Chinese immigrant workers of effective leadership in labor issues.

The lineage tradition of Chinese peasants was another significant determinant of labor activism. In Guangdong Province, from which most New York Chinese originated, a salient feature was that peasants lived in lineages. A Chinese lineage was frequently a formal corporate institution owning property, managing temples, schools, and charity projects, and taking an active part in local government. Under the auspices of neo-Confucian scholars of the Song Dynasty (960-1279), the lineage federated all the families with a common ancestry and in a given location, regardless of whether these families were rich or poor. Lineage leaders even enjoyed such judiciary power as putting an unfilial son to death, which was not usually found in other cultures.

But a significant difference was created by the collective ownership of land in Guangdong. Land inherited from the common ancestors was usually owned by the whole lineage. As table 6.3 indicates, almost half of the cultivated land in

Table 6.3. Proportion of Lineage Land to Total Cultivated Areas in the Eight Counties that Sent Emigrants to the United States, 1933

District	Percent	District	Percent
Taishan	50	Panyu	50
Enping	40	Shunde	60
Kaiping	40	Nanhai	40
Xinhui	60	Zhongshan	50

Source: Han-sheng Chen, *Landlord and Peasant in China: A Study of the Agrarian Crisis in South China*, 34.

the emigrant areas of Guangdong was lineage land. The land belonging to a lineage was rotated among the owners. The tenants who rented the land were most often also rightful owners. Part of the income from the corporate land belonged to the common treasury and was disposed of in the interest of the whole lineage: subsidizing poor members of the lineage, students, and chaste widows; repairing roads, bridges and graves; and performing various kinds of ceremonies. Because each lineage usually inhabited one whole village in Guangdong before the mid-twentieth century, the relationship between the landlord and the tenant was often one between members of the same lineage. As a result, the relationship between the tenant and the landlord was basically characterized by a lack of class consciousness as a result of collective ownership of lineage land.

This is not to say that Chinese peasants were always happy with their situations. Indeed, there were times when the poor peasants' discontent surfaced, but the way in which they righted their wrongs was anything but political. In most cases, rebellions were not directed toward the landowning class, but toward the government whose oppressive policies were regarded as the major cause of poverty among the peasants. In contrast to the southern Italian peasant rebels of the late nineteenth century who often carried the portraits of the King, Jesus Christ, and even Karl Marx during their parades against the rich, the typical goal of a Chinese peasant rebellion was to overthrow the central government and the emperor, not so much the landlords who were mostly their lineage members. The Taiping Rebellion (1850-1864), whose leaders were mostly from Guangdong and its neighboring province Guangxi, preceded the Sicilian Fasci by only a few decades but was in sharp contrast to it. The Taiping rebels' goal was to overthrow the Qing government through a bloody revolution and to replace it with a new dynasty under the control of the rebel leaders. This, in a way, was similar to the Sicilian jacqueries before the mid-1850s. On the whole, Cantonese peasants had never learned to use strikes as a weapon to right their wrongs.

IV

In the case of Italians, the mingling with New York's labor force and the confrontation with the exploitative employers nurtured class consciousness and labor militancy. At the same time, the workplace was also where the New World reality and the Old World traditions interacted upon each other. For those who already had some embryonic class consciousness, the New York experience transformed them into labor militants even faster. This was especially so when the artisans began to preach radicalism to the peasant immigrants. Although in Italy there often existed a gap between the artisans and the contadini, sometimes a connection did develop between the two. Peasants, for example, were frequent customers of artisans' shops and often celebrated the *feste* together with the artisans.[82] In the 1890s, some artisans in Sicily not only established ties to the peasants but also became leaders of the peasant movement.[83] Although these ties were still embryonic and volatile in the Old World, urban congestion and the increasingly similar life pattern in New York brought the two classes closer to each other.[84] Many peasant immigrants, therefore, were able to transcend their half-developed class consciousness and join the labor movement. In fact, many ex-Fasci members became involved in the strikes in American cities.[85]

Although the Chinese transplanted their tradition of tenant-landlord collaboration to the New World, this tradition was not irreversible if these immigrants had a chance to join the mainstream labor force. The militancy they displayed in California and New Jersey suggests that, under similar working conditions, the Chinese could be as militant as their Italian counterparts. Unfortunately, the Chinese were forced to work in the family or quasi-family firms. Rejected by the conservative labor unions and without effective artisan leadership, the Cantonese tradition of class collaboration was allowed to proliferate in those firms. This is why for a long time Chinese immigrants in New York did not become labor militants and were not identified with the American labor movement.

By studying the economic opportunities of the New York Chinese, this study reveals that the level of immigrants' labor militancy—willingness to fight their employers—was as important as the willingness of the established unions to accept them. Because they were faced with exploitative employers, Italian immigrant workers showed labor militancy much earlier than the Chinese. The fact that the Chinese in California and New Jersey demonstrated labor militancy, but in New York they did not, highlights the importance of the employment relationship. They became militant in California and New Jersey because in those places they were hired in large numbers by non-Chinese employers. Later in New York, racial discrimination confined the Chinese to the family or quasi-family firms. As the previous discussion has shown, concentration in small businesses was obstructive to the growth of class consciousness. This argument on the importance of economic opportunity is also reinforced by the labor militancy demonstrated by the Chinese immigrant workers in New York after the 1950s. They became labor militants then because by this time the economic structure of the New York Chinese resembled that of the Italians earlier that century.

But emphasizing the importance of economic opportunity does not imply that the immigrants' heritage was unimportant. Without effective artisan and socialist leadership, the formation of labor militancy among the Italians would almost certainly have been much slower. Similarly, it can be argued that if the proportion of Chinese artisans and skilled workmen had been much larger, Chinese immigrants might have been able to express labor militancy much earlier. The contadini's embryonic class consciousness also seems to have made a difference between the two immigrant groups. Since they already had some experience of staging strikes and associating with the socialists at home, Italian immigrants responded to the radicalism preached by the artisans in New York relatively quickly and favorably. Lack of class consciousness and experience in strikes probably explains why the Chinese organized themselves vertically when they did strike in California in the 1880s. It also explains why the Chinese immigrant workers gave a cold shoulder to the leftists who tried to arouse class consciousness among them in the 1930s.

Notes

This chapter has been published in *Labor History* as an independent article (*Labor History*, fall 1996, Vol. 37, No. 4, 480-99). I wish to thank *Labor History* for permission to reprint the article.

1. See, for example, Barth, *Bitter Strength*, 212.

2. For a discussion of the strikes staged by the Chinese in California and some other western states, see Saxton, *The Indispensable Enemy*, 9-10, 104, 215-18. For information on the strikes launched by the Chinese farm workers in California, see Chan, *This Bittersweet Soil*, 332-33. For information on the strike activities of the Chinese in Hawaii, see Takaki, *Strangers from a Different Shore*, 148-49.

3. Fenton, *Immigrants and Unions*, 24-25, 36-37.

4. See the discussion in chapter 5. See also George Pozzetta, "The Italians of New York City, 1890-1914" (Ph.D. dissertation, University of North Carolina at Chapel Hill, 1971), 342.

5. Fenton, *Immigrants and Unions*, 46.

6. The Federal Writers Project, *The Italians of New York* (New York: Arno Press, 1969), 65.

7. *Il Progresso Italo-Americano*, 10 July 1913, 2 and 6 August 1913, 11 July 1914, and 11 November 1914.

8. Fenton, *Immigrants and Unions*, 197-99. For a discussion of the transience of an Italian butchers' strike in New York, see Pozzetta, "The Italians of New York City," 338-39.

9. Fenton, *Immigrants and Unions*, 208-10.

10. Pozzetta, "The Italians of New York City," 358-59.

11. *United America*, 5 December 1925.

12. *United America*, 9 October 1926.

13. The Federal Writers Project, *The Italians of New York*, 64-65.

14. *Wei Xin Bao*, 26 February 1919 and 7 May 1919.

15. *New York Times*, 6 August 1928.

16. These leftists included some Chinese students and former members of the Kuomintang (the Chinese Nationalist Party). During the early and mid-1920s, the Kuomintang adopted many radical policies in China such as land reform. But toward the end of the 1920s, the KMT began to shift to the right. Discontented with the party's conservatism, some members of the New York branch of the KMT left the party and sought alliance with U.S. leftists such as the Communist Party of the United States. For more information on the Chinese leftists in the 1920s and 1930s, see *Min Qi Ri Bao*, 10 February 1927, and *Xian Feng Bao*, 15 February 1933.

17. *Xian Feng Bao*, 1 July and 1 August 1933.

18. *Xian Feng Bao*, 1 September 1932. The editor was referring to a similar unsuccessful promotion the year before. For a detailed discussion of the failure of the Chinese left to arouse class consciousness among the New York Chinese laundrymen, see Yu, *To Save China, To Save Ourselves*, 56-59. See also Peter Kwong, *Chinatown New York: Labor and Politics, 1930-1950* (New York: Monthly Review Press, 1979), 72-74.

19. *Mei Zhou Hua Qiao Ri Bao*, 23 July 1952 and *Min Qi Ri Bao*, 17 and 21 May 1951.

20. *Mei Zhou Hua Qiao Ri Bao*, 23 July 1952.

21. *Mei Zhou Hua Qiao Ri Bao*, 4, 5, 6 and 7 April 1957.

22. *Mei Zhou Hua Qiao Ri Bao*, 5 March 1958.

23. David Montgomery, *The Fall of the House of Labor: The Workplace, the State, and American Labor Activism, 1865-1925* (New York: Cambridge University Press, 1987), 85-86. For the hostility of the Knights of Labor toward the Chinese, see Philip S. Foner, *History of the Labor Movement in the United States*, Vol. II, *From the Founding of the American Federation of Labor to the Emergence of American Imperialism* (New York: International Publishers, 1955), 58-59.

24. Fenton, *Immigrants and Unions*, 146-47.

25. According to *Wei Xin Bao*'s report, eighty-four New York Chinese restaurant workers signed a statement to withdraw from the IWW. See *Wei Xin Bao*, 26 February 1919.

26. Foner, *History of the Labor Movement*, 59.

27. Foner, *History of the Labor Movement*, 59-60.

28. *New York Times*, 28 May 1893.

29. *New York Times*, 10 March 1895.

30. See *New York Times*, 16 May 1893; D'Alesandre, "Occupational Trends of Italians in New York," 11-21.

31. Charlotte Adams, "Italian Life in New York," *Harper's Magazine*, Vol. 62, No. 371 (April 1881), 676.

32. Fenton, *Immigrants and Unions*, 250, 396, 493.

33. Fenton, *Immigrants and Unions*, 250.

34. Fenton, *Immigrants and Unions*, 198.

35. *Il Progresso Italo Americano*, 21 August 1891.

36. Gary R. Mormino and George E. Pozzetta, *The Immigrant World of Ybor City: Italians and Their Latin Neighbors in Tampa, 1885-1985* (Urbana: University of Illinois Press, 1987), 106, 117, 119-122, 128; Donna Gabaccia, "Neither Padrone Slaves Nor Primitive Rebels, Italians on Two Continents," in *Struggle a Hard Battle*, ed. Dirk Hoerder (DeKalb, Ill.: Northern Illinois University Press, 1986), 106.

37. See, for example, S. T. Chen's article, "A Review of the Situation in the Past Ten Years and a Look into the Future," *Mei Zhou Hua Qiao Ri Bao*, 26 April 1943. (Chen was a leading figure of the Chinese Hand Laundrymen's Alliance of New York.)

38. Lian-ai Tan, "Chinese Laundrymen and Trade Unionism," *Min Qi Ri Bao*, 7 August 1941.

39. Saxton, *The Indispensable Enemy*, 9.

40. Saxton, *The Indispensable Enemy*, 215.

41. A. M. Simons, "The Miners' Union—A Doer of Big Deeds," *Pearson's Magazine*, 37 (February 1917), 132, quoted in Montgomery, *The Fall of the House of Labor*, 335-36. Chinese cannery workers in Alaska also struck in the 1870s, 1880s and 1930s. See Chris Friday, *Organizing Asian American Labor: the Pacific Coast Canned-Salmon Industry,1870-1942* (Philadelphia: Temple University Press, 1994), 38-39, 83-84; Shih-shan Henry Tsai, *The Chinese Experience in America* (Bloomington, Ill.: Indiana University Press, 1986), 109.

42. Saxton, *The Indispensable Enemy*, 215.

43. Fenton, *Immigrants and Unions*, 214.

44. Saxton, *The Indispensable Enemy*, 218; Montgomery, *The Fall of the House of Labor*, 86.

45. *New York Tribune*, 21 June 1885.

46. *Newark (New Jersey) Sunday Call*, 9 October 1932.

47. Ted Brush, "Chinese Labor in North Jersey," *North Jersey Highlander* (Spring 1973), 17, 19-20.

48. Renqiu Yu, *To Save China, To Save Ourselves*, 9-10.

49. See Rose Pesotta, *Bread upon the Waters*, ed. John Nicholas Beffel (Ithaca, N.Y.: ILR Press, New York State School of Industrial and Labor Relations, Cornell University, 1987), 67-77.

50. *Time*, Vol. 31, No. 13, 28 March 1938, 56.

51. Judy Yung, *Unbound Feet*, 215; Shih-shan Henry Tsai, *The Chinese Experience in America*, 109-10; Takaki, *Strangers from a Different Shore*, 252. After making some concessions, however, the owner of the National Dollar Stores closed the factory and the strikers lost their jobs.

52. See Yung, *Unbound Feet*, 212, 215.

53. *New York Times*, 28 June 1967; Kwong, *The New Chinatown*, 147.

54. Gwen Kin Kead, "A Reporters at Large—Chinatown," 71; Kwong, *The New Chinatown*, 151-52.

55. For the situation of the laundry workers, see *Mei Zhou Hua Qiao Ri Bao*, 16 January 1971. No report was made on the result of this demand. For the militancy of the restaurant workers, see Kwong, *The New Chinatown*, 64, 143-44.

56. Kwong, *The New Chinatown*, 64, 143-44.

57. *Mei Zhou Hua Qiao Ri Bao*, 24 February 1965.

58. John J. D'Alesandre, "Occupational Trends of Italians in New York," *Italy-America Monthly*, Vol. 2 (February 25, 1935), 11-21.

59. Gabaccia, "Neither Padrone Slaves Nor Primitive Rebels," 108.

60. Fenton, *Immigrants and Unions*, 261, 269.

61. Fenton, *Immigrants and Unions*, 385.

62. *Il Progresso Italo-Americano*, 2 July 1891.

63. Fenton, *Immigrants and Unions*, 157, 159, 162, 385.

64. Briggs, *An Italian Passage*, 17-18. See also Fenton, *Immigrants and Unions*, 15.

65. Fenton, *Immigrants and Unions*, 13, 16, 19.

66. Fenton, *Immigrants and Unions*, 394.

67. Foerster, *The Italian Emigration of Our Times*, 87.

68. Rudolph Vecoli, "Contadini in Chicago: A Critique of the Uprooted," *Journal of American History*, LIV (1964), 405; Christopher Seton-Watson, *Italy from Liberalism to Fascism*, 23.

69. Leonard Covello, *The Social Background of the Italo-American School Child: A Study of the Southern Italian Family Mores and Their Effect on the School Situation in Italy and America* (Totowa, N.J.: Rowman & Littlefield, 1972), 61.

70. Donna Gabaccia, *Militants and Migrants: Rural Sicilians Become American Workers* (New Brunswick, N.J.: Rutgers University Press, 1988), 44.

71. E. J. Hobsbawm, *Primitive Rebels: Studies in Archaic Forms of Social Movement in the Nineteenth and Twentieth Centuries* (New York: W.W. Norton, 1965), 99.

72. Gabaccia, *Militants and Migrants*, 55; Daniel L. Horowitz, *The Italian Labor Movement* (Cambridge, Mass.: Harvard University Press, 1963), 31-32.

73. Foerster, *The Italian Emigration of Our Times*, 101.

74. The report did not specify what bill it was. Most likely it meant the Chinese Exclusion Act of 1882.

75. *New York Times*, 30 July 1884.

76. *New York Tribune*, 21 June 1885.

77. *Who's Who of the Chinese in New York*, 86.

78. *New York Tribune*, 21 June 1885.

79. United States Government, U.S. Bureau of the Census, *The Fourteenth Census, 1920*, Vol. IV, *Occupations* (Washington, D.C.: Government Printing House, 1922), Chapter VII, "Males and Females in Selected Occupations, New York City," 1161. According to the *Who's Who of the Chinese in New York*, there were six cigarmakers in Chinatown in 1918, see 86.

80. See, for example, John Higham, *Strangers in the Land: Patterns of American Nativism, 1860-1925* (New York: Atheneum, 1981), 72, 161, 162.

81. See Bodnar, *The Transplanted*, 88-89.

82. Gabaccia, *From Sicily to Elizabeth Street*, 51, 55; for more information on the contact between unionists and peasants in south Italy, see Carlo Tresca, *Autobiography* (Minneapolis: Center of Immigration Studies, University of Minnesota), 31, 34-36.

83. Gabaccia, *From Sicily to Elizabeth Street*, 56.

84. Gabaccia, *From Sicily to Elizabeth Street*, 110.

85. Fenton, *Immigrants and Unions*, 16.

7

Conclusion

By examining the effects of the ethnic economy, we can now view the Chinese immigrant experience in New York from a new perspective. It is indeed true that, from the 1890s to the 1960s, racial hostilities toward Chinese in America remained severe. Avoiding and fighting discrimination consequently always was a high priority on the immigrants' agendas. And these Asians were certainly not docile. In 1892, a group of Brooklyn Chinese challenged the implementation of the Geary Act, which required Chinese immigrants to register with the immigration authorities.[1] In 1933, the Chinese laundrymen in New York took collective action, which forced the Board of Aldermen to modify a discriminatory laundry ordinance aimed at Chinese.[2] In 1975, as mentioned earlier, 2,500 New York Chinese demonstrated against the beating of a Chinese American by the fifth precinct police.[3] But protests and demonstrations were just one kind of reaction made by Chinese to the American environment. By contrast, another kind of reaction—making choices for survival—has received little attention from researchers. This study thus represents one of the first efforts to address the problem.

This book has demonstrated that making a living, or simply surviving, was sometimes even more crucial to Chinese immigrants than fighting and avoiding discrimination. Often, their economic situation of depending on work in small businesses required them to act in ways that may have exacerbated the discrimination against them. Consequently, for seven decades, the New York Chinese had to make some difficult choices: whether to live in white neighborhoods or to live among other Chinese in Chinatown; whether to abandon their group allegiances or to retain kinship and regional ties; whether to fight employers or to ignore the labor movement; and whether to return to China in the early 1950s or to stay in the United States.

Apparently, each alternative involved advantages and drawbacks. Contrary to what conventional wisdom often assumes, the majority of the New York Chinese chose to live in white neighborhoods, to maintain their group allegiances, and not to return to China in the early 1950s. They made such

Table 7.1. Survival Choices for the New York Chinese, 1890s to 1950s

Economic	Risk of Racist Attack	
Survival	High	Low
Probability		
High	I	II
Low	III	IV

choices not because they believed that the discrimination they experienced would abate. But because economic marginalization had left them with only one area for survival, in laundries and restaurants, they knew their situation would have been even worse—they would have starved—had they chosen to do otherwise. After the 1950s, the concentration of employment in, along with owning and running, small laundries and restaurants gave way to the enclave economy in New York's Chinatown. New economic opportunity allowed the New York Chinese to make different survival choices than those they had made before the 1960s. Now more and more of them took up residence in Chinatown. They no longer tenaciously adhered to the regional and kinship networks as they had before the 1960s, and they began to unionize and to fight their employers when mistreated. In sum, the New York Chinese made different choices for their survival over time depending on what kind of ethnic economy they engaged in.

By revealing that racial hostilities alone cannot solve such problems as the immigrants' return migration, residential location choices, and group loyalties, this book does not intend to slight the effects of racial hostilities against Chinese (on the contrary, it demonstrated many instances of racial hostilities against the Chinese in New York). Nor does it intend to shift to a new monistic approach to Chinese American history by viewing the ethnic economy as the sole factor at work affecting the immigrants' adjustment. Rather, the book offers a new perspective for understanding the complicated relationship between racial hostilities and economic survival. As table 7.1 indicates, before the mid-1960s, the interaction between racial hostilities and the need for economic survival involved four different situations. Situation I represents the case in which Chinese laundrymen worked and lived in white neighborhoods, and the New York Chinese decided to stay in America after 1950. In this case, they ran high risks of racist attacks, but enjoyed a higher probability of economic survival. Situation II involves the businesses mainly catering to Chinese customers, such as Chinese grocery stores and druggists. These firms mainly located in Chinatown proper. The situation also concerns the pattern of remigration: Most New York Chinese intended to return to China before 1950. Situation II was obviously a favorable scenario for the New York Chinese: For the businesses catering mainly to Chinese customers, to locate their firms in Chinatown not only meant better business opportunities but also enabled their workers to live in the enclave to avoid discrimination in white neighnorhoods. For those who went back to Guangdong before 1950, the return migration promised them two advantages: avoiding on-going discrimination in the United States and living a better life at home.

Situations III and IV were obviously undesirable for the New York Chinese. If, for example, owners of Chinese grocery stores located their firms in white vicinities, they would not only run high risks of racist attack but also distance themselves from the best business location—Chinatown. Similarly, although to locate their laundries in Chinatown would enable the laundrymen to avoid outside discrimination, the probability of economic survival would certainly be very low since in this case they would be almost out of touch with their mainly white customers. The fact that very few New York Chinese were found in situations III and IV suggests that the need for economic survival was even more crucial than avoiding racial hostilities. Scholars of the economic sociology of immigration argue that immigrants are rational actors "pursuing goals through deliberately selected means."[4] The New York Chinese were obviously rational actors who compared the different options available to them and made their choices primarily for their own survival.

Whether or not racial hostilities and the need for economic survival worked in the same direction would heavily influence the way in which we understand the history of the New York Chinese. When the two factors moved together, such as in encouraging the New York Chinese to return home before 1950 (situation II) or, if some Chinese New Yorkers ever tried, in locating their grocery stores and druggists in white neighborhoods (situation III), we may easily adopt a monistic approach. Under such circumstances, it is indeed tempting to focus our attention solely on racial hostilities but overlook the need for economic survival because racial violence was more visible. Because the two factors moved together, to overlook one of them—the need for survival—may seem insignificant. And this monistic approach still seems capable of explaining why the New York Chinese refrained from situation III and why some of them adhered to situation II. But problems arise when racial hostilities and the need for survival moved in different directions. As we have shown, such a monistic approach cannot explain why the New York Chinese decided to stay in America in the early 1950s when racial discrimination against them remained rampant, and why most of them chose to live in white neighborhoods despite severe racial hostilities there. Apparently, we can provide satisfactory answers to these questions only by taking both racial hostilities and the need for survival into consideration. The arguments here strongly suggest that a pluralistic perspective is more useful and more effective in explaining the Chinese American experience than monistic approaches. But although it has discovered the essential role played by economic survival, this book does not view ethnic economy as the sole factor affecting the immigrants' lives. Indeed, a pluralistic approach represented by this book always welcomes new perspectives added to the picture.

This book also opens a useful perspective for understanding the differences between various Chinese American communities. Scholars often treated the New York Chinese history as an isolated case. They seldom linked the Chinese experiences in New York to those in other cities. As a result, we may easily assume that the Chinese experiences in all American cities were identical. We may further assume so if we believe that racial hostilities were an exclusive factor shaping the lives of Chinese immigrants. The brief comparisons developed in this book indicate that indeed that was not the case. Between the San Francisco and New York Chinese communities significant differences existed. While the San Francisco Chinese concentrated in Chinatown most of the time, their New York counterparts were far more widely scattered throughout the five boroughs. Group loyalties among the San Francisco Chinese, furthermore, began to decline several decades earlier than those among their East Coast brethren. Another major difference concerns the timing when labor militancy emerged: Those West Coast Chinese began striking against their employers as early as 1938 but similar situations did not occur in New York until the 1970s.

Apparently, ethnic heritage alone can lead only to the conclusion that the Chinese experiences in different American cities were identical. Racial hostilities alone can not fully explain these differences, either. It would be simplistic, for example, to attribute the earlier abandonment of group loyalties by the San Francisco Chinese and their concentration in Chinatown to more discrimination on the West Coast. But in the case of New York City and San Francisco, racial hostilities against Chinese were indeed difficult to quantify, this was especially so after 1890 when large-scale anti-Chinese movements on the West Coast basically subsided. As mentioned earlier, the anti-Chinese racial discourse started in New York City decades earlier than in San Francisco. The press and politicians in New York kept up harangue about the undesirability of Chinese throughout the nineteenth century and well into the twentieth. The Chinese Exclusion Act, furthermore, was enforced everywhere in the United States, New York as well as San Francisco. Economically, the New York Chinese were even less lucky than their San Francisco brethren. Therefore, the post-1890 differences between the two Chinese communities could hardly be explained by the more racial hostilities on the West Coast. Under such circumstances, economic opportunities, especially the situation of the workplace, may become a meaningful bridge that links our understanding of Chinese experiences in New York with those in other American cities such as San Francisco. Though further studies are certainly needed to explore the different adjustment patterns of the San Francisco and New York Chinese, we may cautiously advance the following hypothesis: Because an enclave economy emerged earlier among the San Francisco Chinese than among their counterparts in New York, the adjustment patterns of the Chinese in the two metropolitan areas became significantly different. In the case of San Francisco, due to their manufacturing nature and large size, Chinese garment factories could concentrate in Chinatown, could hire large numbers of workers from different regional and kinship backgrounds, and allowed the confrontation between capital and labor to develop. As a result, group loyalties declined sooner and class solidarity developed faster in the San Francisco Chinese community.

The brief discussion of the Italian immigration experience provides a useful point of reference. Although institutionalized racism was a crucial factor distinguishing the two immigrant groups' experiences, other factors, especially the need for economic survival, were by no means unimportant. The Italian experience reminded us of the importance of economic opportunities, especially in the situation of the workplace, and of the leading role of artisans in affecting the immigrants' adjustment. Economic opportunities, indeed, may become an important new perspective in understanding the different adjustment patterns of European and Asian immigrants. In comparison with the Italians, group loyalties remained stronger and class consciousness developed more slowly among the New York Chinese before the 1960s. These differences, as this study has demonstrated, were not just the result of institutionalized discrimination against Chinese, but they were also caused by the fact that the Chinese had been confined to working in small laundries and restaurants for too long.

Notes

1. *New York Times*, 21 August 1892.
2. Kwong, *Chinatown New York*, 63-66.
3. *New York Times*, 13 May 1975.
4. Portes ed. *The Economic Sociology of Immigration*, 3.

Appendix

Tables

Table A.1. Chinese Arrivals in and Departures from United States, 1882-1892

Year Ending June 30	Imm.	Chinese Arrivals in U.S. Non-Imm.	Total	Chinese Departures from U.S. All classes
1882	39,579	— —	39,579	10,366
1883	8,031	2,151	10,182	12,159
1884	279	3,194	3,473	14,145
1885	22	5,330	5,352	19,655
1886	40	4,809	4,849	17,591
1887	10	3,754	3,764	12,155
1888	26	2,751	2,777	12,893
1889	118	1,945	2,063	10,226
1890	1,716	154	1,870	8,056
1891	2,836	171	3,007	8,924
1892	2,728	462	3,190	6,696

Source: U.S. Bureau of Census, *Historical Statistics of the United States, 1789-1945* (Washington, D.C., 1949). Cited in Shih-Shan Henry Tsai, *The Chinese Experience in America* (Bloomington, Ind.: Indiana University Press, 1986), 194.

Table A.2. Country of Birth of the Foreign-born Population of the United States, 1850-1930

Country of Birth	1850	1860	1870	1880	1890
Italy	3,679	11,677	17,157	44,230	182,580
China	758	35,565	63,042	104,468	106,701

1900	1910	1920	1930
484,027	1,343,125	1,610,113	1,790,429
81,534	56,756	43,560	46,129

Source: *The Fifteenth Census, 1930*, Vol. I, 233.

Table A.3. Major Occupational Groups of the Chinese in the United States by Decade and Percent, 1940-1970

Major Occupation Groups	1940	1950	1960	1970
Total Employed	36,454	48,409	98,784	181,190
Professional/Technical	2.8%	7.1%	17.9%	26.5%
Managers	20.6%	19.8%	12.7%	8.9%
Sales Workers	11.4%	15.9%	6.6%	4.3%
Clerical Workers	11.4%	15.9%	13.8%	16.8%
Craftsmen	1.2%	2.9%	5.2%	5.4%
Operators	22.6%	17.1%	15.0%	14.8%
Laborers, except farmers	0.7%	1.7%	1.3%	2.3%
Farmers	3.8%	2.6%	1.0%	0.6%
Service Workers	30.4%	28.8%	18.8%	19.6%
Private Household Workers	6.2%	2.6%	1.0%	0.8%
Not Reported	0.3%	1.5%	6.5%	— —

Source: U.S. Census Bureau, *Decennial Censuses* (1940, 1950, 1960, 1970). Cited in Tsai, *The Chinese Experience in America*, 195.

Table A.4. Chinese Population for New York State and New York City, 1880-1960

Year	New York State	New York City
1880	909	747
1890	2,935	2,048
1900	7,170	6,321
1910	5,266	4,614
1920	5,793	5,042
1930	9,665	8,414
1940	13,731	12,753
1950	20,171	18,327
1960	37,573	32,831

Source: *The Tenth Census, 1880*, 547; *The Eleventh Census, 1890*, 637; *The Fourteenth Census, 1920*, Vol. III, *Population*, 676, 679; *The Fifteenth Census, 1930*, Vol. III, *Population*, Part II, 297; *The Sixteenth Census, 1940*, Vol. II, *Population*, 157; *The Seventeenth Census, 1950*, Vol. II, *Population*, Part 32, 56, 171; *The Eighteenth Census, 1960*, Vol. I, 100, and Vol. II, *Population*, Part 34, 51.

Table A.5. Number and Nationalities of Immigrants Arrived in the United States, 1860-1905

	Country	
Year	China	Italy
1860	6,117	920
1865	3,702	594
1870	15,740	2,893
1875	16,437	3,631
1880	5,802	12,354
1885	22	13,642
1890	1,716	52,003
1895	539	35,427
1900	1,247	100,135
1905	2,166	221,479

Source: *Annual Report of the Immigration Commission*, 1905, 38-41.

Table A.6. Distribution of Foreign-born Italian Americans in the United States and New York State Exhibiting New York State Ratio & New York City Ratio by Decade, 1900-1970

Year	United States	New York State	Ratio	New York City Portion
1900	484,703	182,248	.38	.30
1910	1,343,125	472,201	.35	.25
1920	1,610,113	545,173	.34	.24
1930	1,790,429	629,322	.35	.25
1940	1,623,580	584,075	.36	.25
1950	1,427,145	503,175	.35	.24
1960	1,255,812	440,063	.35	.28
1970	1,005,687	352,711	.35	.21

Source: U.S. Department of Commerce, *Decennial Census*, 1900-1970, cited in *New York City's Italians: Census Characteristics at a Glance*, ed. Edward J. Miranda and Ino J. Rossi (New York: Italian-American Center for Urban Affairs, Inc., 1976), 8.

138

Table A.7. Number of Foreign-born Italians
in New York State and New York City by
Decade, 1900-1970

Year	New York State	New York City
1900	182,248	145,433
1910	472,192	340,322
1920	545,173	390,832
1930	629,322	440,250
1940	584,075	409,489
1950	503,175	344,115
1960	440,063	345,489
1970	352,711	212,160

Source: U.S. Department of Commerce, *Decennial Census*, 1900-1970, cited in *New York City's Italians: Census Characteristics at a Glance*, ed. Edward J. Miranda and Ino J. Rossi (New York: Italian-American Center for Urban Affairs, Inc., 1976), 8.

Table A.8. Italian Immigration to New
York City by Year, 1900-1925

Year	Number	Year	Number
1900	30,041	1913	66,386
1901	40,799	1914	70,935
1902	53,513	1915	12,422
1903	69,187	1916	8,416
1904	57,988	1917	8,649
1905	66,444	1918	1,313
1906	81,936	1919	471
1907	85,719	1920	23,786
1908	38,551	1921	55,565
1909	54,965	1922	10,080
1910	53,884	1923	11,669
1911	45,721	1924	12,562
1912	39,284	1925	1,489

Source: *New York City's Italians: Census Characteristics at a Glance*, ed. Edward J. Miranda and Ino J. Rossi (New York: Italian-American Center for Urban Affairs, Inc., 1976), 16.

Character List

Baohuanghui 保皇會
Bendi (Punti) 本地

Changle 長樂
Changping 常平
Chaoan 潮安
Chaoyang 潮陽
Chen-Hu-Yuan Family
　Association 至孝篤親公所
Chenghai 澄海
Chongzheng Hui Guan 崇正會館
Conghua 從化

Dabu 大埔
Dapeng Hui Guan 大鵬同鄉會
Deng-Cen-Ye Family
　Association 南陽
　(鄧岑葉)公所
Dongan Hui Guan 東安公所
Dongguan 東莞

Enping 恩平
Enping Hui Guan 恩平會館
Enping Xian Zhi 《恩平縣誌》

Fang 房
Fangcheng 防城
Fengshun 豐順
Foshan 佛山
Fujian 福建
Fujian Hui Guan 福建同鄉會
Fuzhou 福州

Gaoyao 高要
Guangdong (Kwangtung) 廣東
Guangxi 廣西
Guangxu 光緒
Guangzhou (Canton) 廣州
Guo Quan Bao 《國權報》
Haiyan Hui Guan 海晏同鄉會

He Shen 和珅
Heshan 鶴山
Heshan Hui Guan 鶴山會館
Hong Xiu Quan 洪秀全
Hua Bei Hui Guan 華北同鄉會
Hua Gong Chu Guo Shi Liao Hui
　Bian
　《華工出國史料匯編》
Huangbu (Wampoa) 黃埔
Huaxian 花縣
Hubei 湖北
Hui Guan 會館
Hui Shen 慧深
Huiyang 惠陽
Huizhou Hui Guan 惠州工商會

Jia Qing 嘉慶
Jiangsu-Zhejiang-Jiangxi Hui
　Guan 三江公所
Jiaoling 蕉嶺
Jiaying 嘉應
Jieyang 揭陽

Kaiping 開平
Kaiping Hui Guan 開平會館
Kaiping Xin Zhi 《開平縣誌》
Kang You-wei 康有為
Kejia (Hakka) 客家

Kuomintang 國民黨

Lechang 樂昌
Lei-Fang-Kuang Family
　Association 溯源公所
Lian Cheng Gong Suo 聯成公所
Liang Qi-chao 梁起超
Lin Family Association
　林河西堂
Lin Ze Xu 林則徐
Lu Mei San Yi Zong Hui Guan

Jian Shi
《旅美三邑總會館簡史》
Luoding 羅定

Maoming 茂名
Mei Zhou Hua Qiao Ri Bao
《美州華僑日報》
Meixian 梅縣
Min Qi Ri Bao 《民氣日報》
Mu 畝

Nanhai 南海
Nanhai-Shunde Hui Guan
南順同鄉會
Nanhai Xian Zhi 《南海縣誌》
Nanjing (Nanking) 南京
Ningpo 寧波
Niu Yue Hua Qiao She Hui
《紐約華僑社會》

Panyu 番禺
Panyu Hui Guan 番禺同鄉會
Pingyuan 平遠

Qian Long 乾隆
Qing (Ch'ing) 清
Qingyuan 清遠
Quanzhou 泉州
Qujiang 曲江

Raoping 饒平

San Yi 三邑
San Zhou Ri Ji 《三洲日記》
Shaanxi 陝西
Shunde 順德
Si Yi 四邑
Sichuan 四川
Song (Sung) 宋
Tai Ping Rebellion 太平天國
Taishan 台山
Taishan-Ningyang Hui Guan
台山寧陽會館
Taishan Xian Zhi 《台山縣誌》
Tan-Tan-Xu-Xie Family

Association
昭倫(譚談許謝)公所
Tang 唐
Tianjin (Tientsin) 天津

Wangxia 望廈
Wei Xin Bao 《維新報》
Wongyuan 翁源
Wuchuan 吳川

Xiamen 廈門
Xian Feng Bao 《先鋒報》
Xiao Fang Hu Zhai Yu Di Cong
Chao
《小方壺齋輿地叢鈔》
Xin Bao 《新報》
Xinan 新安
Xingning 興寧
Xinhui 新會
Xinhui Hui Guan 新會同鄉會
Xinhui Xian Zhi 《新會縣誌》
Xinyi 信宜
Xue-Situ Family Association
鳳倫公所

Yangjiang 陽江
Ye Jianying 葉劍英
Yingde 英德
Yu Family Association 余風采堂

Zhang Yinhuan 張蔭桓
Zhongshan 中山
Zhongshan Hui Guan
中山同鄉會
Zhu Family Association
朱沛國堂

Bibliography

Newspapers and Magazines

Atlantica (1923-1937)
Catholic World (1888, 1895, 1900)
Century Magazine (August 1899)
Charities (1899-1946)
Forum (1886-1930)
Guo Quan Bao (*Chinese Republic News*) (1917-1938)
Harper's Weekly (1880-1916)
Il Progresso Italo-Americano (1886-1925)
Italy-America Monthly (1934-1935)
Mazzini News (1941-1941)
Mei Zhou Hua Qiao Ri Bao (*China Daily News*) (1940-1970)
Min Qi Ri Bao (*Chinese Nationalist Daily*) (1927-1958)
New York Times (1853-1990)
New York Tribune (1888-1912)
Saturday Evening Post (1951)
Time, Vol.31, March (1938)
United America (1925-1928)
Wei Xin Bao (*Chinese Reform News*) (1904-1934)
Xian Feng Bao (*Chinese Vanguard*) (1932-1938)
Xin Bao (*China Tribune*) (1943-1946)

Government Documents

Annals of the Chinese Economy (Nanjing, China, 1928)
Bureau of the Census, Department of Commerce, *Census Reports*
Chinese Exclusion Files
Economic Facts (Nanking, China, 1936-1946)
Reports of the Immigration Commission (after the 1930s the Immigration and Naturalization Service)
The Statutes At Large of the United States of America

Autobiographies, Memoirs, and Historical Novels

Beck, Louis J. *New York's Chinatown: A Historical Presentation of Its People and Places.* New York, 1898.

Brandenburg, Broughton. *Imported Americans: The Story of the Experiences of a Disguised American and His Wife Studying the Immigration Question.* New York, 1904.

Chu, H. Louis. *Eat A Bowl of Tea.* Seattle. 1961.

Corrensca, Rocco. "The Biography of a Bootblack." *Independent,* No. 5 (December 4, 1902).

Corsi, Edward. *In the Shadow of Liberty.* New York, 1935.

Covello, Leonard. *The Heart Is the Teacher.* New York, 1958.

D'Agelo, Pascal. *Son of Italy.* New York, 1924.

Donato, Pietro di. *Christ in Concrete.* New York, 1939.

Giacosa, Giuseppe. *Impressioni d'America.* Milano, 1898.

Gibson, Otis. *The Chinese in America.* Cincinnati, 1877.

Glick, Carl. *Shake Hands with the Dragon.* New York, 1941.

————. *Three Times I Bow.* New York, 1943.

Kinkead, Gwen. "A Reporter at Large: Chinatown." *The New Yorker,* June 10, 1991.

LaGuardia, Fiorello H. *The Making of an Insurgent: An Autobiography, 1882-1919.* Philadelphia, 1948.

LaGumina, Salvatore. *The Immigrants Speak: Italian Americans Tell Their Story.* New York, 1981.

Leong, Gor Yun. *Chinatown Inside Out.* New York, 1936.

Leung, Sin Jang. "A Laundryman Sings the Blues." Trans. Marlon K. Hom. In *Chinese America: History and Perspectives,* 1991.

Morrison, Joan. *American Mosaic: The Immigrant Experience in the Words of Those Who Lived It.* New York, 1980.

Panunzio, Constantine M. *The Soul of an Immigrant.* New York, 1969.

Pesotta, Rose. *Bread Upon the Waters.* Ed. John Nicholas Beffel. Ithaca, 1987.

Riis, Jacob. *How the Other Half Lives: Studies among the Tenements of New York.* New York, 1901.

Rossi, Adolfo. *Un Italiano in America.* Milano, 1894.

Tresca, Carlo. *Autobiography.* University of Minnesota, Immigration History Research Center,.

Tsiang, H. T. *And China Has Hands: An Odyssey of a Chinese Coolie.* New York, 1937.

Wong, Chin Foo. "The Chinese in New York." *Cosmopolitan,* Vol. 5, No. 4 (June 1888).

Wong, Jade Snow. *Fifth Chinese Daughter.* New York, 1950.

Directories, Local Chronicles, and Special Bulletins

Bulletin of the 32nd Anniversary of the Chinese Laundry Association, Inc., New York, 1966.

Bulletin of the 50th Anniversary of the Chinese Chamber of Commerce of New York, Inc., New York, 1957.

Bulletin of the Chinese-American Restaurant Association of New York, New York, 1975.

Bulletin of the 100th Anniversary of the Founding and 58th Anniversary of the Naming of the First Chinese Presbyterian Church in the City of New York, 1868-1968, New York, 1968.

Chinese Hand Laundry Alliance 5th Anniversary Special Bulletin, New York, 1938.

Directory of Italian and Italian-American Organizations and Community Services in the Metropolitan Area of New York, Vol. 2, New York, 1980.

Directory of the Chinese in the Eastern Cities, New York, 1958.

Enping Xian Zhi (Chronicles of Enping).

Kaiping Xian Zhi (Chronicles of Kaiping).

Nanhai Xian Zhi (Chronicles of Nanhai).

New York Chinese Business Directory, New York, 1984.

Xinhui Xian Zhi, (Chronicles of Xinhui).

Xinning Xian Zhi (Chronicles of Taishan).

Books

Aquilano, Baldo. *L'Ordini Figli D'Italia in America*. New York, 1926.

Banfield, Edward. *The Moral Basis of a Backward Society*. New York, 1958.

Bard, Emile. *Chinese Life in Town and County*. New York, 1905.

Barth, Gunther. *Bitter Strength: A History of the Chinese in the United States, 1850-1870*. Cambridge, Mass., 1964.

Barton, Josef. *Peasants and Strangers: Italians, Rumanians, and Slovaks in an American City, 1890-1950*. Cambridge, Mass., 1975.

Bayor, Ronald H. *Neighbors in Conflict: The Irish, Germans, Jews, and Italians of New York City, 1929-1941*. Baltimore, 1978.

Bell, Rudolph M. *Fate and Honor, Family and Village: Demographic and Cultural Change in Rural Italy Since 1880*. Chicago, 1979.

Blum, John et al. *The National Experience: A History of the United States*. Fort Worth, Tex., 1993.

Bodnar, John. *The Transplanted: A History of Immigrants in Urban America*. Bloomington, 1985.

Bogen, Elizabeth. *Immigration in New York*. New York, 1987.

Bonacich, Edna, and John Modell. *The Economic Basis of Ethnic Solidarity: Small Business in the Japanese American Community.* Berkeley, 1980.

Bonner, Arthur. *Alas! What Brought Thee Hither? The Chinese in New York, 1800 to 1950.* Madison, 1997.

Briggs, John W. *An Italian Passage: Immigrants to Three American Cities, 1890-1930.* New Haven, 1978.

Burnham, Walter D. *The Current Crisis in American Politics.* New York, 1982.

Chan, Sucheng. *Asian Americans: An Interpretive History.* Boston, 1991.

———. *Entry Denied: Exclusion and the Chinese Community in America, 1882-1943.* Philadelphia, 1991.

———. *This Bittersweet Soil: The Chinese in California Agriculture, 1860-1910.* Berkeley, 1986.

Chen, Han-sheng. *Landlord and Peasant in China: A Study of the Agrarian Crisis in South China.* New York, 1936.

———. ed. *Hua Gong Chu Guo Shi Liao Hui Bian (A Collection of Sources of Chinese Emigration),* 6 volumes. Beijing, 1981.

Chen, Hsiang-shui. *Chinatown No More: Taiwan Immigrants in Contemporary New York.* Ithaca, 1992.

Chen, Jack. *The Chinese of America: From the Beginnings to the Present.* San Francisco, 1981.

Chen, Ta. *Emigrant Communities in South China: A Study of Overseas Emigration and Its Influence on Standard of Living and Social Change.* Shanghai, 1939.

Cheng, Lucie, and Edna Bonacich. *Labor Immigration under Capitalism: Asian Workers in the United States before World War II.* Berkeley, 1984.

Chinatown Study Group. *Chinatown Report 1969.* New York, 1970.

Chinn, Thomas W., ed. *A History of the Chinese in California: A Syllabus.* San Francisco, 1969.

Cinel, Dino. *From Italy to San Francisco: The Immigrant Experience.* Stanford, 1982.

Clough, Shepard B. *The Economic History of Modern Italy.* New York, 1964.

Cohen, Warren I. *America's Response to China: A History of Sino-American Relations.* New York, 1990.

Cordasco, Francesco. *Studies in Italian American Social History.* Totowa, N.J., 1975.

Cordasco, Francesco, and Eugene Bucchioni, eds. *The Italians: Social Background of an American Group.* Clifton, N.J., 1974.

Covello, Leonard. *The Social Background of the Italo-American School Child: A Study of the Southern Italian Family Mores and Their Effect on the School Situation in Italy and America.* Totowa, N.J., 1972.

Daniels, Roger. *Asian America: Chinese and Japanese in the United States since 1850.* Seattle, 1988.

DeConde, Alexander. *Half Bitter, Half Sweet: An Excursion into Italian*

American History. New York, 1971.

di Leonardo, Micaela. *The Varieties of Ethnic Experience: Kinship, Class, and Gender among California Italian Americans.* Ithaca, N.Y., 1984.

Diggins, John P. *Mussolini and Fascism: The View from America.* Princeton, 1972.

Dinnerstein, Leonard, Roger L. Nichols, and David M. Reimers. *Natives and Strangers: Ethnic Groups and the Building of America.* New York, 1979.

Fairbank, John King. *China: A New History.* Cambridge, Mass., 1994.

———. *China: Tradition and Transformation.* Boston, 1989.

———. *Trade and Diplomacy on the China Coast : The Opening of the Treaty Ports, 1842-1854.* Cambridge, Mass., 1964.

The Federal Writers. *The Italians of New York.* New York, 1969.

Fenton, Edwin. *Immigrants and Unions, A Case Study: Italians and American Labor, 1870-1920.* New York, 1975.

Foerster, Robert E. *The Italian Emigration of Our Times.* Cambridge, Mass., 1924.

Foner, S. Philip. *History of the Labor Movement in the United States,* Vol. II: *From the Founding of the American Federation of Labor to the Emergence of American Imperialism.* New York, 1955.

Freedman, Maurice. *Lineage Organization in Southeast China.* London, 1958.

———. *Chinese Lineage and Society: Fukien and Kwangtung.* New York, 1966.

Friday, Chris. *Organizing Asian American Labor: The Pacific Coast Canned-Salmon Industry, 1870-1942.* Philadelphia, 1994.

Gabaccia, Donna. *We Are What We Eat: Ethnic Food and the Making of Americans.* Cambridge, Mass., 1998.

———. *From Sicily to Elizabeth Street: Housing and Social Change among Italian Immigrants, 1880-1930.* Albany, N.Y., 1984.

———. *Militants and Migrants: Rural Sicilians Become American Workers.* New Brunswick, N.J.,1988.

Gerber, David A. *The Making of an American Pluralism: Buffalo, New York, 1825-1860.* Urbana, Ill., 1989.

Gist, Noel P., and Sylvia F. Fava. *Urban Society.* New York, 1964.

Glick, Clarence E. *Sojourners and Settlers: Chinese Migrants in Hawaii.* Honolulu, 1980.

Glazer, Nathan, and Daniel Moynihan. *Beyond the Melting Pot: The Negroes, Puerto Ricans, Jews, Italians, and Irish of New York City.* Cambridge, Mass., 1963.

Gordon, David M., Richard Edwards, and Michael Reich. *Segmented Work, Divided Workers: The Historical Transformation of Labor in the United States.* Cambridge, England, 1982.

Green, David. *From Artisans to Paupers: Economic Changes and Poverty in London, 1790-1870.* Aldershot, England, 1995.

Greene, Victor R. *American Immigrant Leaders, 1800-1910.* Baltimore, 1987.

Hatamiya, Leslie T. *Righting a Wrong: Japanese Americans and the Passage of the Civil Liberties Act of 1988.* Stanford, Calif. 1993.

Herberg, Will. *Protestant, Catholic, Jew.* Garden City, N.Y., 1960.

Higham, John. *Strangers in the Land: Patterns of American Nativism, 1860-1925.* New York, 1981.

Ho, Ping-ti. *A Historical Survey of Landsmannschaften in China.* Taipei, 1966.

Hobsbawm, E. J. *Primitive Rebels: Studies in Archaic Forms of Social Movement in the 19th and 20th Centuries.* New York, 1965.

Hoerder, Dirk, ed. *Struggle a Hard Battle.* New York, 1986.

Horowitz, Daniel. *The Italian Labor Movement.* Cambridge, Mass., 1963.

Hourwich, Isaac A. *Immigration and Labor.* New York, 1969.

Hsu, Francis L.K. *Americans and Chinese: Passage to Differences.* Honolulu, 1985.

———. *The Challenge of the American Dream: The Chinese in the United States.* Belmont, Calif. 1971.

Hunt, Michael H., *The Making of a Special Relationship : The United States and China to 1914.* New York, 1983.

Kessner, Thomas. *The Golden Door: Italian and Jewish Immigrant Mobility in New York City, 1880-1915.* New York, 1977.

Kulp, Daniel H. *Country Life in South China: The Sociology of Familism.* New York, 1925.

Kuo, Chia-ling. *Social and Political Change in New York's Chinatown: The Role of Voluntary Associations.* New York, 1977.

Kwong, Peter. *Chinatown New York: Labor and Politics, 1930-1950.* New York, 1979.

———. *Forbidden Workers: Illegal Chinese Immigrants and American Labor.* New York, 1997.

———. *The New Chinatown.* New York. 1987.

Kusmer, Kenneth L., ed. *Black Communities and Urban Development in America, 1720-1990.* New York, 1991.

LaGumina, Salvatore J. *Ethnicity in American Political Life: The Italian American Experience.* New York, 1968.

Laurie, Bruce. *Artisans into Workers: Labor in Nineteenth-Century America.* New York, 1993.

Lee, Rose Hum. *The Chinese in the United States of America.* Hong Kong, 1960.

Light, H. Ivan. *Ethnic Enterprise in America: Business and Welfare among Chinese, Japanese and Blacks.* Berkeley, 1972.

Liu, Hui-chen Wang. *The Traditional Chinese Clan Rules.* Locust Valley, N.Y., 1959.

Lyman, Stanford. *The Asian in North America.* Santa Barbara, Calif. 1977.

———. *Chinese Americans.* New York, 1974.

Mariano, John H. *Italian Contribution to the American Democracy*. Boston, 1921.

McClain, Charles J. *In Search of Equality: The Chinese Struggle against Discrimination in Nineteenth-Century America*. Berkeley, 1994.

Miller, Stuart C. *The Unwelcome Immigrant: The American Image of the Chinese, 1785-1882*. Berkeley, 1971.

Miranda, Edward J., and Ino J. Rossi. *New York City's Italians: Census Characteristics at a Glance*. New York, 1976.

Mormino, Gary R., and George E. Pozzettaa. *The Immigrant World of Ybor City: Italians and Their Latin Neighbors in Tampa, 1885-1985*. Urbana, 1987.

Montgomery, David. *The Fall of the House of Labor: The Workplace, the State, and American Labor Activism, 1865-1925*. New York, 1987.

Nee, Victor G. and Brett de Bary, *Longtime Californ': A Documentary Study of an American Chinatown*. Stanford, 1972.

Nelli, Humbert S. *From Immigrants to Ethnics: The Italian Americans*. New York, 1983.

———. *Italians in Chicago, 1880-1930: A Study in Ethnic Mobility*. New York, 1970.

Odencrantz, Louise. *Italian Women in Industry: A Study of Conditions in New York*. New York. 1919.

Orsi, Robert A. *The Madonna of 115th Street: Faith and Community in Italian Harlem, 1880-1950*. New Haven, 1985.

Osofsky, Gilbert. *Harlem: The Making of a Ghetto, Negro New York, 1890-1930*. Chicago, 1996.

Pan, Erica Y.Z. *The Impact of the 1906 Earthquake on San Francisco's Chinatown*. New York, 1995.

Pan, Lynn. *Sons of the Yellow Emperor: A History of the Chinese Diaspora*. New York, 1994.

Park, Robert E., and Herbert A. Miller, eds. *Old World Traits Transplanted*. New York, 1969.

Parmet, Robert D. *Labor and Immigration in Industrial America*. Boston, 1981.

Pernicone, Nunzio. *Italian American Radicalism: Old World Origins and New World Development*. Proceedings of the 5th Annual Conference of the American Italian Historical Association, New York, 1972.

Perry, Elizabeth. *Shanghai on Strike: The Politics of Chinese Labor*. Stanford, 1993.

Portes, Alejandro. *The Economic Sociology of Immigration: Essays on Networks, Ethnicity, and Entrepreneurship*. New York, 1995.

Purcell, Victor. *The Chinese in Southeast Asia*. London, 1965.

Sandmeyer, Elmer Clarence. *The Anti-Chinese Movement in California*. Urbana, Ill., 1973.

Safley, Thomas Max, and Leonard N. Rosenband, eds. *The Workplace before*

the Factory, Artisans and Proletarians, 1500-1800. Ithaca, N.Y., 1993.
Salvemini, Gaetano. Italian Fascist Activities in the United States. New York, 1977.
Saxton, Alexander. The Indispensable Enemy: Labor and the Anti-Chinese Movement in California. Berkeley, 1971.
Schaffer, Allan. Vito Marcantonio, Radical in Congress. Syracuse, N.Y., 1966.
Schirokaurer, Conrad. A Brief History of Chinese and Japanese Civilizations. New York, 1978.
Schneider, Jane, and Peter Schneider. Culture and Political Economy in Western Sicily. New York, 1976.
Seton-Watson, Christopher. Italy from Liberalism to Fascism, 1870-1925. Frome and London, 1967.
Skinner, G. William. Chinese Society in Thailand: An Analytical History. Ithaca, N.Y., 1957.
Smith, Judith. Family Connections: A History of Italian and Jewish Immigrant Lives in Providence, Rhode Island, 1900-1940. Albany, N.Y., 1985.
Spear, Allan H. Black Chicago: The Making of a Negro Ghetto, 1890-1920. Chicago, 1967.
Sung, Betty Lee. The Adjustment Experience of Chinese Immigrant Children in New York City. New York, 1987.
———. Chinese American Intermarriage. New York, 1990.
———. Mountain of Gold: The Story of the Chinese in America. New York, 1967.
———. A Survey of Chinese-American Manpower and Employment. New York, 1976.
Takaki, Ronald. Strangers from a Different Shore: A History of Asian Americans. New York, 1989.
Tchen, John. New York before Chinatown: Orientalism and the Shaping of American Culture, 1776-1882. Baltimore, 1999.
Tien, Ju-kang. The Chinese of Sarawak: A Study of Social Structure. London, 1953.
Thomson, James C. Jr., Peter W. Stanley, and John Curtis Perry. Sentimental Imperialists: The American Experience in East Asia. New York, 1981.
Tomasi, S. M., and M. H. Engel, eds. The Italian Experience in the United States. New York, 1970.
Tomasi, Silvano M. Piety and Power: The Role of the Italian Parishes in the New York Metropolitan Area, 1880-1930. New York, 1975.
Tomasi, Silvano, ed. Perspectives in Italian Immigration and Ethnicity. New York, 1977.
Tricarica, Donald. The Italians of Greenwich Village. New York, 1984.
Tsai, Shih-shan Henry. The Chinese Experience in America. Bloomington, 1986.
———. China and the Overseas Chinese in the United States, 1868-1911. Fayetteville, Ark., 1983.

Tung, William L. *The Chinese in America, 1820-1973: A Chronology and Fact Book.* Dobbs Ferry, N.Y., 1974.

Von Norden, Warner M.,ed. *Who's Who of the Chinese in New York.* New York, 1918.

Wakeman, Frederick. *Strangers at the Gate: Social Disorder in South China, 1839-1861.* Berkeley, 1966.

Wang, Gungwu. *The Chinese Overseas: From Earthbound China to the Quest for Autonomy.* Cambridge, Mass., 2000.

———. *China and Chinese Overseas.* Hong Kong, 1994.

Wang, L. Ling-chi and Gungwu Wang, eds. *The Chinese Diaspora: Selected Essays.* Singapore, 1998.

Ware, Caroline. *Greenwich Village, 1920-1930: A Comment on American Civilization in the Post-War Years.* Boston, 1935.

Wong, Bernard. *A Chinese American Community: Ethnicity and Survival Strategies.* Singapore, 1979.

Wu, Chen Tzu, ed. *Chink! A Documentary History of Anti-Chinese Prejudice in America.* New York, 1972.

Yans-McLaughlin, Virginia. *Family and Community: Italian Immigrants in Buffalo, 1880-1930.* Ithaca, N.Y., 1977.

———, ed. *Immigration Reconsidered: History, Sociology, and Politics.* New York, 1990.

Yen, Ching-huang. *Coolies and Mandarins: China's Protection of Overseas Chinese during the Late Ching Period, 1851-1911.* Singapore, 1985.

———. *A Social History of the Chinese in Singapore and Malaya, 1800-1911.* Singapore, 1986.

Yu, Renqiu. *To Save China, To Save Ourselves: The Chinese Hand Laundry Alliance of New York.* Philadelphia, 1992.

Yuan, D.Y. *Chinese American Population.* Hong Kong, 1988.

Yung, Judy. *Unbound Feet: A Social History of Chinese Women in San Francisco.* Berkeley, 1995.

Zhang, Jiang-ming. *Li Shi Zhuan Zhe Shi Ke de Ye Jian Ying (Ye Jian Ying at the Historical Turning Point).* Beijing, 1997.

Zhou, Min. *Chinatown: The Socioeconomic Potential of an Urban Enclave.* Philadelphia, 1992.

Articles

Baily, Samuel. "The Adjustment of Italian Immigrants in Buenos Aires and New York, 1870-1914." *The American Historical Review,* Vol. 88, No. 2 (1983).

Chan, Sucheng. "European and Asian Immigration into the United States in Comparative Perspective, 1820s to 1920s." In *Immigration Reconsidered, History, Sociology, and Politics,* ed. Virginia Yans-McLaughlin, New York:

1990.

Cohen, Mariam. "Changing Education Strategies among Immigrant Genera-
tions: New York Italians in Comparative Perspective." *Journal of Social
History*, Vol. 15, No. 3 (1982).

————. "Italian-American Women in New York City, 1900-1950: Work and
School." In *Class, Sex, and the Woman Worker*, ed. Milton Cantor. New
York, 1977.

Daniels, Roger. "American Historians and East Asian Immigrants." In *The
Asian American: The Historical Experience*, ed. Norris Hundley Jr., Santa
Barbara,1976.

————. "Westerners from the East: Oriental Immigrants Reappraised." *Pacifica
Historical Review*, Vol. XXXV, No. 4 (1966).

Gabaccia, Donna. "Kinship, Culture and Migration: A Silician Example."
Journal of American Ethnic History, spring 1984.

————. "Little Italys Decline: Immigrant Renters and Investors in a Changing
City." In *The Landscape of Modernity: Essays on New York City, 1900-
1940*, ed. David Ward and Olivier Zunz. New York, 1992.

————. "Neither Padrone Slaves Nor Primitive Rebels: Italians on Two
Continents." In *Struggle A Hard Battle*, ed. Dirk Hoerder. New York, 1986.

Green, Nancy J. "Sweatshop Migration: The Garment Industry between Home
and Shop." In *The Landscape of Modernity*, ed. Ward and Zunz.

Ianni, Francis A. J. "Familialism in South Italy and in the United States." In
Perspectives in Italian Immigration and Ethnicity. ed. S. M. Tomasi. New
York, 1977.

Kennedy, Rudy. "Single or Triple Melting Pot? Intermarriage Trends in New
Haven, 1870-1940." *The American Journal of Sociology*, Vol. XLIX, No. 4
(January 1944).

Lan, Dean. "Chinatown Sweatshops." In *Counterpoints: Perspectives on Asian
America*, ed. Emma Gee. Los Angeles, 1976.

Lau, Ivonne. "Traditionalism and Change in a Chinese-American Community."
In *The Chinese in America*, ed. Paul K.T. Sih and Leonard B. Allen. New
York, 1976.

Ma, L. Eve Armentrout. "Chinatown Organizations and the Anti-Chinese
Movement, 1882-1914." In *Entry Denied*, ed. Sucheng Chan.

MacDonald, J. S. "Agricultural Organization: Migration and Labor Militancy in
Rural Italy." *The Economic History Review*, 2nd. Series, No. 16 (1963).

Mei, June. "Socioeconomic Origins of Emigration: Guangdong to California,
1850-1882." In *Labor Immigration under Capitalism: Asian Workers in the
United States before World War II*, ed. Lucie Cheng and Edna Bonacich.
Berkeley, 1984.

Moore, Deborah Dash. "On the Fringes of the City: Jewish Neighborhoods in
Three Boroughs." In *The Landscape of Modernity*, ed. Ward and Zunz.

Murphey, Rhoads. "Boston's Chinatown." *Economic Geography*, Vol. XXVIII,

No. 3 (July 1952).

Ng, Franklin. "The Sojourner, Return Migration, and Immigration History." In *Chinese America: History and Perspectives*. 1987.

Olneck, Michael R., and Marvin Lazerson. "The School Achievement of Immigrant Children, 1900-1930." *History of Education Quarterly*, Vol. 14 (winter, 1974).

Orsi, Robert. "The Fault of Memory: 'Southern Italy' in the Imagination of Immigrants and the Lives of Their Children in Italian Harlem, 1920-1945." *Journal of Family History*, Vol. 15 (1990).

Peffer, George A. "Forbidden Families: Emigration Experiences of Chinese Women under the Page Law, 1875-1882." *Journal of American Ethnic History*, fall 1986.

Pozzetta, George. "The Mulberry District of New York City: The Years before World War One." In *Little Italys in North America*, ed. Robert F. Harney and J. Vencenza Scarpaci. Toronto, 1981.

Stephens, John W. "A Quantitative History of Chinatown, San Francisco, 1870 and 1880." In *the Life, Influence and the Role of the Chinese in the United States, 1776-1960*. Proceedings/Papers of the National Conference held at the University of San Francisco, July 10-12, 1975. San Francisco, 1976.

Tang, Mei-chun. "On the Political Functions of the Chinese Familial Institution." *Bulletin of the College of Liberal Arts*, Taiwan University, No. 27 (December 1978).

Tchen, John Kuo Wei. "New York Chinese: The Nineteenth-Century Pre-Chinatown Settlement." In *Chinese America: History and Perspectives*. January 1990.

Vecoli, Rudolph. "Contadini in Chicago: A Critique of the Uprooted." *Journal of American History*. No. LIV (1964).

———. "Prelates and Peasants: Italian Immigrants and the Catholic Church." *Journal of Social History*, Vol. 2 (spring 1969).

Wong, Bernard. "Elites and Ethnic Boundary Maintenance: A Study of the Role of Elites in Chinatown, New York." *Urban Anthropology*, Vol. 16 (1977).

Wong, K. Scott. "Liang Qichao and the Chinese of America: A Re-evaluation of His Selected Memoir of Travels in the New World." *Journal of American Ethnic History*, Vol. II, No. 4 (summer 1992).

Yuan, D.Y. "Chinatown and Beyond: The Chinese Population in Metropolitan New York." *Phylon*, Vol. XXVII, No. 4 (winter 1966)

Dissertations and Theses

Beardry, James Amand. "Acculturation and Assimilation: Chinese Professionals in Upstate New York." Ph.D. dissertation, Cornell University, 1966.

Chen, Julia. "The Chinese Community in New York, 1920-1940." Ph.D.

dissertation, American University, 1941.

Heyer, Virginia. "Patterns of Social Organizations in New York's Chinatown." Ph.D. dissertation, Columbia University, 1953.

Liang, Yuan. "The Chinese Family in Chicago." Master's thesis, University of Chicago, 1951.

Pozzetta, George. "The Italians of New York City, 1890-1914." Ph.D. dissertation, University of North Carolina at Chapel Hill, 1971.

Pratt, Edward E. "Industrial Causes of Congestion of Population, New York City." Ph.D. dissertation, Columbia University, 1911.

Russo, Nicholas. "The Religious Acculturation of the Italians of New York." Ph.D. dissertation, St. John's University, 1968.

Wu, Cheng-tsu. "Chinese People and Chinatown in New York City." Ph.D. dissertation, Clark University, 1958.

Index

About the Author

Xinyang Wang received his Ph.D. in social history from Yale University. He is a member of the Division of Humanities at the Hong Kong University of Science & Technology. Prior to joining the faculty at HKUST, he taught at Washington State University. His articles and reviews have appeared in *Labor History*, *New York History*, *Western Historical Quarterly*, and *Amerasia Journal*. Currently, he is working on another book which compares the Chinese immigrant experiences in the United States and in southeast Asia.